The Stifled Soul of Humankind

Paul Cudenec

For all my friends in France.

Published by Winter Oak Press, Sussex, England

winteroak@greenmail.net

Cover art by Dieric Bouts the Elder

ISBN: 978-0-9576566-2-8

CONTENTS

	Preface	**vii**
I	The Dispossessed	**1**
II	Cultural Resistance	**16**
III	Underground Freedom	**26**
IV	Disenchanted Lives	**36**
V	From Prophets to Profits	**43**
VI	Creative Block	**67**
VII	Romantic Revolutionaries	**75**
VIII	The World Soul	**88**
IX	Total Rejection	**101**
X	A Crime Against Humanity	**114**
XI	The Spiral of Hope	**123**
	Endnotes	**132**

PREFACE

My previous writing has started from the point most familiar to me, and presumably to my readers – the society in which we today find ourselves living. I have tried to describe what is fundamentally wrong with it and have suggested ways in which we might, individually and collectively, try to bring about the enormous transformation that will be required to stave off a grim future of human enslavement and environmental devastation. In this book, I take a more historical approach, illustrating my overview by sketching out some of the paths through which humanity has reached the sorry state into which it has descended in the early decades of the 21st century. I did briefly ask myself if the "humankind" of the title wasn't too sweeping a term, when the subject matter is mainly western European civilization, but this latter entity is responsible, through colonialism past and present, for a thoroughly global stifling of our spirit.

There is a certain thematic overlap with my previous work, which is perhaps inevitable when the subject matter is basically the same! Reality is too complex and multi-faceted to be described in one take and my various essays could be seen as a series of two-dimensional snapshots which, when combined, hint at the shape of a multi-dimensional reality.

The motivating vision behind all this could perhaps best be described as an attempt to strip away all the detailed distraction of contemporary politics and reveal the centuries-old foundations of the injustice which surrounds us. It is, I would maintain, only by seeing and communicating this bigger picture that we can hope ever to change it. By falling into the trap of dealing with the symptoms of our social malaise, rather than the real root causes, we bolster the illusion that there is nothing *essentially* wrong with capitalist civilization and that a certain amount of tinkering would be enough to make it acceptable to one and all. The status quo is always keen to tell us that revolution is impossible and that the best we can hope for is reform – it thus encourages potential revolutionaries to instead follow a broadly liberal agenda. The message I aim to convey in this book, as elsewhere, is that there is an urgent need not to *improve* capitalist society – by making it *nicer* in some way – but to destroy it entirely, along with all the psychological and metaphysical assumptions on which it is built. On that possibility alone rests all the hope of both humankind and the planet.

As I have been living in France while writing this book, many of the texts I cite were originally in French. I have not tried to access English versions, so all translations from French-language titles are my own, even if perfectly good translations already exist. My thanks to everyone at my local anarchist library for making so many useful books available to me in my research and to my friends in Sussex and Scotland for their advice and encouragement.

I

THE DISPOSSESSED

"I was born upon the prairie, where the wind blew free and there was nothing to break the light of the sun. I was born where there were no enclosures and where everything drew a free breath. I want to die there and not within walls".[1] These were the words of Parra-Wa-Samen (Ten Bears) of the Yamparika Comanches. For his people, as Dee Brown explains, "land came from the Great Spirit, was as endless as the sky and belonged to no man".[2] Here, surely, is an unchanging truth. Land is the surface of the Earth, which is billions of years old. How can it be said to be "owned" by transient individuals of one particular species temporarily populating its surface? And yet the huge majority of human beings born today find themselves denied the natural right to live and breathe freely on the planet on which they are born – of whose living substance, indeed, they are part.

The shocking depth of this dispossession is difficult for us to fully understand, from our limited perspective inside the very pit of this reality. It is also hard for us to grasp how we have slipped to this low point and how we have stayed there for so long. It is not difficult to imagine, of course, that there once might have been greedy, violent men (perhaps women, too!) who wanted to grab land for their own selfish use and exclude others. But, first, there must have been the idea that, contrary to the oldest traditions, land was not simply part of nature but could "belong" to somebody in particular. Before the greedy men could desire to own it for themselves, there must have been a novel conception of land as being "ownable". How did that happen? And then, once they had made their move and claimed an area for themselves and their kin, why did everyone else, the majority after all, let them get away with it? How did their theft become permanent? Crucially, at what point was their theft no longer seen as theft? At what point did it appear to be right and proper – so right and proper, in fact, that any attempt to undo this original theft would itself be considered a crime?

Ultimately, we are talking here about the origins of authority, which cannot be separated from the idea of land – the abstract notion of authority backs up the possession of land and thus wealth, while the possession of wealth provides the physical resources to enforce that authority in its real incarnation. How did Authority (with a capital 'A'), as a force in its own right, come to pervert human society in this way? We will consider its metaphysical aspects later in these pages (*Chapter 10*), but for the meantime all we need to know is that somehow, tragically, the land thieves got away with it. Over the centuries, people forgot that the land once belonged to nobody – *could* belong to nobody – and accepted the twin lies that not only did it indeed belong to somebody, but also that the persons who "owned" the land did so *fairly*.

Nowhere was this enforced forgetting more advanced than in Britain, a thoroughly corrupt little kingdom whose malevolent influence on world history was for centuries totally disproportionate to its size and natural wealth. Here, the historic theft of land from the Great Spirit, or the collective community if you prefer, intensified with waves of land enclosures, which began in 1230 and peaked in the 1790s. There were, of course, always a few perceptive dissidents who could see clearly what was happening and were brave enough to denounce it, notably Gerrard Winstanley, a spokesman for The Diggers, who tried to reclaim for the people a small patch of land in Surrey in 1649, the year that the English Revolution took the head of Charles I. He told the landed class, in one of his characteristic broadsides, that "the power of enclosing land and owning property was brought into the creation by your ancestors by the sword; which first did murder their fellow creatures, men, and after plunder or steal away their land, and left this land successively to you, their children. And therefore, though you did not kill or thieve, yet you hold that cursed thing in your hand by the power of the sword; and so you justify the wicked deeds of your fathers, and that sin of your fathers shall be visited upon the head of you and your children to the third and fourth generation, and longer too, till your bloody and grieving power be rooted out of the land".[3] He had no difficulty in seeing through the layers of deceit justifying "ownership" of the land, declaring: "The poorest man hath as true a title and just right to the land as the richest man... True freedom lies in the free enjoyment of the earth".[4]

Throughout the enclosures, there was constant resistance from the population – which is why the process took so long to complete. E.P. Thompson relates that such protests "could be massive and very violent, as was the dispute in Sheffield in 1791. A private act had been passed to enclose six thousand acres of common and waste adjacent to the town, compensating the poor with two acres only. This precipitated spectacular riots... The enclosure commissioners were mobbed; the debtors' gaol was broken open and the prisoners released; there were cries of 'No King!' and 'No Taxes!'".[5] A parallel process, though much more suddenly and severely imposed, took place in the Highlands of Scotland, where clearances of people to make room for sheep, and then deer, occurred in two main periods, from 1782 to 1820 and then from 1840 to 1854. Here too, there was resistance, which – like the Sheffield uprising – became a deeper rebellion in the face of repression. John Prebble records one such instance on the island of North Uist in 1849, in which "black flags of defiance"[6] flew over a township as the crowds gathered to confront the authorities.

However, the Highland rebels, like the English rebels against enclosure, were up against a rapidly developing system whose armoury included not only the physical force to put down internal opposition but also the arrogance to insist that it had the right to do so. A key to its tightening control was the theoretical concept of "property". Every square inch had to be "owned" by somebody. Thompson describes how "in the late seventeenth century and certainly in the eighteenth the courts increasingly defined (or assumed without argument) that the lord's waste or soil was his personal property, albeit restrained or curtailed by the inconvenient usages of custom".[7] Gradually there was "a hardening and concretion of the notion of property in land, and a re-ification of usages into properties which could be rented, sold or willed".[8] The idea of there being any space, anywhere, that was *not* somebody's "property" was regarded as unthinkable and dangerous. For instance, an official report in 1851 complained that the New Forest in southern England "has not, and cannot have, an owner" and this meant that its present state was "little less than absolute anarchy".[9]

This theoretical assumption of necessary land ownership was not confined to Britain, but applied theoretically to the rest of the world as well. "The concept of exclusive property in land, as a norm to which other practices must be adjusted, was now extending across the whole globe, like a coinage reducing all things to a common measure," writes Thompson. "The concept was carried across the Atlantic, to the Indian sub-continent, and into the South Pacific, by British colonists, administrators, and lawyers, who, while not unaware of the force of local customs and land systems, struggled to construe these within their own measure of property".[10] The notion of Property, with a capital 'P', became an ideal in itself – those who gained from its enforcement understood only too well that it was the foundation on which all their power and wealth was based, as is apparent in the words of Lord Portland, Britain's Home Secretary, in the 1790s. He warned: "If the employment of Property is not secure, if every Man does not feel that he has power to retain what he possesses so long as he pleases and dispense it at the time, in the manner and for the Price he chuses to fix upon it, there must be an end of Confidence in Industry and of all valuable and virtuous Exertions of all descriptions... the whole Order of things must be overturned and destroyed".[11]

To the original lies of the possibility of land ownership, and the rightfulness of specific claims, was thus added another lie – that of a pressing moral imperative behind it. The Highland Clearances were referred to, by the ruling classes, as "improvements" and a similar justification was cited for the general enclosure of common land which, it was argued, would be put to more productive use for the benefit of all. Of course, the point of view behind this approach was very specifically that of those who stood to gain from it. The motivation was really economic, rather than moral, and the benefits would accrue not to the community as a whole, but to the rich. The so-called "idleness" of the population was used as an excuse to evict them from land that could profitably be exploited.

This line of argument was easily exported from the Fenlands of England or the Highlands of Scotland to the vast expanses of North America in the 1870s. Calling for the native people to be thrown off the land, right-wing editor and politician William B. Vickers wrote in the *Denver Tribune*: "The Utes are actual, practical Communists and the government should be ashamed to foster and encourage them in their idleness and wanton waste of property".[12] There was, needless to say, a certain subtext behind the reference to the Utes' "wanton waste of property" – as Brown says, the aim of Vickers and his friends was "to push them off those twelve million acres of land waiting to be dug up, dammed up and properly deforested so that fortunes could be made in the process".[13]

Behind the very idea of personal "ownership" of land lies the desire to exclude others from it – otherwise, it would not be such an attractive proposition for would-be profiteers. But increasingly there was another important factor motivating the elite's urge to throw the people off their land: like the earth, the human population was (and is!) regarded as a resource to be exploited to the full. Rural people living simple but happy lives were not only depriving the landowner of exclusive use of the land he claimed to "own", but were also denying to the ruling class the financial fruits of their labour-unit potential in industrial mills and factories. This was not quite how it was phrased, of course. Christopher Hill notes that a book written in 1663 argued that, thanks to the wonders of enclosure, "people were added to the manufacturing population who previously did not increase the store of the nation but wasted it".[14] This was not about increasing the wealth of the rich, note, but that of the "nation", that perpetually convenient cloak for the greed and self-interest of the few!

Since one of the main aims of enclosure was, as Hill remarks, to "force men to sole dependence on wage labour, which many regarded as little better than slavery",[15] they were persistently hounded off the land with an array of laws, enforced with the usual violence where necessary. A statute of 1589 made it a crime to build any cottage without at least four acres of land – a blatant attempt to socially cleanse the countryside of poorer people.[16] The vagrancy Act of 1656 was directed against "all wandering persons" – there was no escaping the embryonic industrial system by living free in the countryside. For the same purposes, gleaning – the simple gathering of the fruits of nature which had been part of human life since the origins of the species – was now treated as "theft". Describing a 1788 court case against a couple accused of this heinous crime, Thompson comments: "It is difficult to think of a purer expression of capitalist rationality, in which both labour and human need have disappeared from view, and the 'natural justice' of profits has become a reason at law. In the arguments of *Steele v Houghton et Uxor* we see exposed with unusual clarity the law's complicity with the ideology of political economy, its indifference to the claims of the poor, and its growing impatience with coincident use-rights over the same soil. As [Lord] Loughborough had it: 'the nature of property... imports exclusive enjoyment'. And how could enjoyment be exclusive if it did not command the power to exclude from property's physical space the insolent lower orders?"[17]

It is worth spelling this out carefully, in order to appreciate the full insidiousness of what was happening. Not only were people being thrown off the land, because they got in the way of money-making "improvements", but they were also being deliberately deprived of their sustenance in order to make them *need* money to buy food and thus be forced into paid labour, from which the ruling classes could extract yet more profit.

The tightening of the screws was systematic and relentless. People were forced to become part of a system which grew fatter and stronger by exploiting them. Yves Delhoysie describes how, as early as the Middle Ages, nobles would order peasants' hand mills destroyed so that they would be forced to take their grain to the nobles' own mills – paying, of course, the relevant charges.[18] Resentment at the stranglehold exercised by millers – middle-men between the people and their food supply – was still in evidence in the 1700s. "Mills were the visible, tangible targets of some of the most serious urban riots of the century", reports Thompson.[19] Meanwhile, seventeenth-century England saw stricter enforcement of game laws, in case the poor managed to maintain some semblance of freedom that way. Writes Hill: "After 1671 *gamekeepers* had the right to search houses and confiscate weapons. The concentration of power in the hands of the landed class could hardly have been better illustrated. Enclosure and the game laws deprived cottagers of many of their traditional sources of food".[20]

The Utes in North America also had to be deprived of their simple-living liberty and forced to adopt "civilized habits" like working for money, according to Nathan C. Meeker, US government agent at the White River Ute reservation from 1878. He complained: "What we call conveniences and comforts are not sufficiently valued by them to cause them to undertake to obtain them by their own efforts".[21] The answer, he felt, was to take away the Utes' hundreds of ponies so that they could no longer roam and hunt, replacing them with a few draft horses for ploughing and hauling. Then, as soon as the Utes were thus forced to abandon the hunt and remain near the reservation, he would stop issuing rations to those who would not reduce themselves to labouring: "I shall cut every Indian down to the bare starvation point, if he will not work".[22] We see here a deliberate global policy in action. As Los Amigos de Ludd observe, while the emerging world order liked to depict itself as representing reason and liberty, it was in fact shamelessly destroying each and every area of human autonomy.[23] The result of this was to force millions of people into what really amounted to slavery – not the manacled inhuman slavery of the plantation worker, it is true, but a slavery born of the fact that working for another's profit became the only way to survive, once access to the land and its gifts had been denied.

Anarchist thinker Peter Kropotkin bemoans the fact that the son of a Western worker "comes into the world more destitute than a savage... Everything has been appropriated by somebody; he *must* accept the bargain, or starve".[24] And he goes right to the nub of the question when he asks: "Who would sell his labor power for less than it is capable of bringing in if he were not forced thereto by the threat of hunger?"[25] As his fellow anarchist Gustav Landauer concludes: "All ownership of things, all land-ownership is in reality ownership of men. Whoever withholds the earth from others, from the masses, forces these others to work for him. Private ownership is theft and slave-holding".[26]

But how is this slavery maintained, how is it that the mass of our fellow humans do not rise up and shake off their chains? Part of the answer is that the activity of "work" has been confused in the dominant mindset by some idea of goodness and we have thus lost sight of the reality of our debased status of dependent servitude. William Morris sees clearly that employment often amounts to nothing more than "slaves' work – mere toiling to live, that we may live to toil".[27] And he reflects: "Most people, well-to-do or not, believe that, even when a man is doing work which appears to be useless, he is earning his livelihood by it – he is 'employed' as the phrase goes; and most of those who are well-to-do cheer on the happy worker with congratulations and praises, if he is only 'industrious' enough and deprives himself of all pleasure and holidays in the sacred cause of labour. In short, it has become an article of the creed of modern morality that all labour is good in itself – a convenient belief to those who live on the labour of others".[28] From their opposite perspective, the ruling classes also occasionally admit that the need for the mass of people to work, simply in order to live, is not at all an issue of morality, but of the survival of a parasitical system. Thus Lord Goderich, the British Colonial Secretary, remarked in 1831 with reference to Upper Canada: "Without some division of labour, without a class of persons willing to work for wages, how can society be prevented from falling into a state of almost primitive rudeness, and how are the comforts and refinements of a civilized life to be procured?"[29]

Apart from this pseudo-morality around working for a living, so helpfully promoted by protestant Christianity and its "work ethic", the main reason why wage-slavery persists is so obvious it need hardly be stated: violence. Violence was used to force people off the land, whether in England, Scotland, North America, India or Africa. Violence is still being used for the same purposes all over the world. It is used to maintain exploitation and keep people in slave-labour conditions so the rich can continue to prosper at their expense. It is also constantly used to attack the slightest sign of any general mass resistance to the rule of a system which was created by theft and perpetuated by force. Examples are too numerous to need citing.

And yet this visible violence, ubiquitous though it is in both historical and contemporary terms, is nothing more than the tip of an iceberg. Erich Fromm describes the crucial importance of *psychological* methods in "leading the masses to a situation of attachment and spiritual dependence with regard to the dominant class or its representatives, in such a way as they submit and obey even without the use of violence".[30] Thompson makes the same point in terms of a cultural hegemony which "induces exactly such a state of mind in which the established structures of authority and modes of exploitation appear to be in the very course of nature. This does not preclude resentment or even surreptitious acts of protest or revenge; it does preclude affirmative rebellion".[31]

Instead of *actual* physical violence, therefore, it is often the *threat* of violence which serves to protect land theft, exploitation and wage slavery. Although the threat is real, and the violence is always in the air and sometimes inflicted, its unremitting brutality is hidden behind the symbolic level on which it is presented on a daily basis. Thompson sees this threat as coded in the very appearance and behaviour of the ruling classes, in this case the gentry of 18th century England: "Their appearances have much of the studied self-consciousness of public theatre. The sword was discarded, except for ceremonial purposes; but the elaboration of wig and powder, ornamental clothing and canes, and even the rehearsed patrician gestures and the hauteur of bearing and expression, all were designed to exhibit authority to the plebs and to exact from them deference. And with this went certain ritual appearances: the ritual of the hunt; the pomp of assizes (and all the theatrical style of the law courts); the segregated pews, the late entries and early departures, at church".[32] Expanding on this aspect of Authority, and the threat of violence on which it depends, he adds: "A great part of politics and law is always theatre; once a social system has become 'set', it does not need to be endorsed daily by exhibitions of power (although occasional punctuations of force will be made to define the limits of the system's tolerance)".[33]

There is one principal form in which this theatricality of violence is acted out, in which a thuggish physical threat, an enforced submission, is presented as acceptable and morally commendable behaviour: the law. Essentially, the law is no more than the codification, the elaboration, of the original theft of land. It is the justification, dreamt up retrospectively, for the enormous crime carried out against humankind by those who were happy to reduce their fellows to servitude in the pursuit of their own material self-indulgence. Kropotkin rightly defines the law as "nothing but an instrument for the maintenance of exploitation and the domination of the toiling masses by rich idlers"[34] and says law and capital are like twins who "have advanced, hand in hand, sustaining one another with the suffering of mankind".[35] Like the abstract ideas of Property and Authority, Law (with a capital 'L') becomes fetishised, held up as some kind of moral god to be worshipped and obeyed regardless of context.

The resistance to the clearances in the Scottish Highlands was therefore not just an "assault on the sacred rights of property"[36] but also, as Sheriff Donald Macleod of Geanies complained in 1792, "an actual, existing Rebellion against the Laws".[37] Lord Justice-Clerk Hope, jailing two rebellious Highlanders in 1854, declared: "The course of the Law must have its effect with all, in order to protect all persons high and low; and all must submit whatever their feelings, or rank, or perverted notions of right and wrong, to the authority of the Law... Neither they nor their neighbours can be allowed to suppose that they can live in this kind of wicked and rebellious spirit against the Law. They must be taught submission in the very first instance".[38]

Submission is here presented as the opposite of wickedness. Submission to the theft of land (very real and contemporary in this instance) is decreed morally good behaviour – as morally good, perhaps, as spending one's life working for somebody else's profit. Crime, taking on the guise of Authority, thus sets itself up as the unique source of moral judgement in an extension of the series of interdependent monopolies it builds up around itself to establish its complete hegemony.

What began as the aftermath of a theft becomes a self-legitimising reality that seemingly can never be challenged, let alone changed. The culture tells us that this is how things *have* to be, always have been and always *must* be. In Franz Kafka's novel *The Trial,* we are told the story of a man from the countryside who asks for admittance to the Law but is told to wait, by an intimidating-looking door-keeper, an incarnation of the theatricality of Authority. The door-keeper tells him: "If you are so strongly tempted, try to get in without my permission. But note that I am powerful. And I am only the lowest door-keeper. From hall to hall, keepers stand at every door, one more powerful than the other. And the sight of the third man is already more than even I can stand".[39] The man from the country doesn't try to get past the first door-keeper, but waits in vain outside the door for the rest of his life. As Michael Löwy comments: "The man from the country has let himself be intimidated: it isn't force that stops him from going in but fear, a lack of self-confidence, false obedience to authority, submissive passivity".[40] It may well have been true that if the man *had* tried to get inside, he would have been stopped and even killed by those guarding the Law. The physical force at the disposal of Authority is not necessarily an illusion. But by failing to challenge it, by failing to test its physical strength, he makes it easier for it to maintain the lie that it does not in fact rule by violence, but by general consent to its moral rightness and inevitability.

In this way the ruling classes build up a structure of power in which the violence at its core is hidden by an arrangement of mirrors, reflecting back to each other their unfounded claim to moral right. Property and Authority are legitimate in terms of Law. Law is established by Authority. Authority is built on and resourced by Property. Property is secured and protected by Law which, with the blessing of Authority, also threatens or deploys violence against anyone wicked and rebellious enough to challenge the whole scam. There is a name given to this tangled knotwork of theft and lies which protects and perpetuates the criminal behaviour of what is currently the ruling elite. We call it the State.

We can turn again to Kropotkin for a clear definition of this entity: "The State was established for the precise purpose of imposing the rule of the landowners, the employers of industry, the warrior class, and the clergy upon the peasants on the land and the artisans in the city. And the rich perfectly well know that if the machinery of the State ceased to protect them, their power over the laboring classes would be gone immediately".[41] Moral deceit has always been at the centre of the State's existence. "The state lies in all languages of good and evil," says Friedrich Nietzsche. "Whatever it says, it lies – and whatever it has, it has stolen".[42]

Today, another of the State's big lies is the notion of "democracy", which is in truth nothing but an extension of the original fabricated "moral right" dressed up with the phoney symbolic mechanisms of so-called representation and used as further self-justification of the system and its use of repression to maintain its dictatorship. Tom Anderson explains in a 2013 study: "The 'rule of law' serves to protect capitalist interests, in the name of public order, security and democracy. By using labels such as 'terrorist' and 'domestic extremist', particular forms of activity can be cast as beyond the pale, as having crossed the line from legitimate dissent into criminal activity. Meanwhile, activity which does not fundamentally challenge or disrupt the structures of capitalism can be promoted as proof of societies' 'democratic' nature... the ability to define 'legal' and 'illegal' provides a crucial means by which political dissent is channelled into 'legitimate' forms which do not fundamentally threaten capitalist interests, while dissent which cannot be channelled or co-opted is criminalised and rendered illegitimate, pernicious and therefore deserving of repression".[43]

What we must never forget is that the State – with its associated concepts of Property, Authority and Law – has never left behind the violence on which it was built, no matter how cleverly it tries to hide it away behind all the theatrical institutions and self-referential assumptions that make up its culture of control. George Granville Leveson-Gower, Marquess of Stafford, Duke of Sutherland, was proud to be known as The Great Improver. He was the richest landowner in Britain, with more than a million acres and tens of thousands of tenants bringing a massive annual income of £300,000. He was "the product of a class to whom Property was becoming a sacred trust and its improvement an obligation that must take precedence over all others". This class, argues Prebble, "sincerely believed that its own enrichment must bring a greater good to a greater number".[44]

And yet, although they may have often found it comfortable to float in this bubble of sanctimonious delusion, Stafford and the other lairds came to know full well that "they could count upon the full power of the Law, backed by bayonets if necessary, to support them in removing their tenants and replacing them with sheep".[45] Betsy Mackay was 16 years old in 1814, when she and her family were violently evicted from their ancestral homes on the Stafford estates. She later recalled: "The people had to escape for their lives, some of them losing all their clothes except what they had on their backs. The people were told they could go where they liked, provided they did not encumber the land that was by rights their own. The people were driven away like dogs who deserved no better".[46]

Similar scenes were still being acted out 40 years later, when the women of Strathcarron resisted evictions in 1854. Remembered Donald Ross: "The police struck with all their force... not only when knocking down, but after the females were on the ground. They beat and kicked them while lying weltering in their blood. Such was the brutality with which this tragedy was carried through, that more than twenty females were carried off the field in blankets and litters, and the appearance they presented with their heads cut and bruised, their limbs mangled and their clothes clotted with blood, was such as would horrify any savage".[47]

Here is the reality behind the "improvements" carried out by Stafford, behind the "sacred trust" and the moral "obligation" he was supposedly fulfilling. Here is the reality behind Property, the "rule of law" and the power of Authority. Here is the reality behind Order, Progress and Civilization. As Bakunin says of the State, that guarantor and incarnation of all these interconnected violations and falsehoods, essentially it is "nothing else but the negation of humanity".[48]

II

CULTURAL RESISTANCE

Look around you and see the gentry
with no pity for the poor creatures,
with no kindness to their kin.
They do not think that you belong to the land,
and although they leave you empty
they do not see it as a loss.[1]

This 18th century reflection on the Highland Clearances, by the bard Ian MacCodrum, points to another aspect of land theft beyond those considered in the last chapter: people are not only materially, but also culturally, dispossessed. "Enclosure, in taking the commons away from the poor, made them strangers in their own land",[2] as E.P. Thompson observes. When communities were denied use of the land which had always nurtured them, they were also being cut off from the culture that came with it.

Christopher Hill notes that "the royal policy of disafforestation and enclosure, or of draining The Fens, as applied before 1640, involved disrupting a way of life, a brutal disregard for the rights of commoners: they and their children were often deprived of old-established playing areas".[3]

Natural surroundings provide a rich and healthy background for children's ontogeny, as discussed elsewhere,[4] and create adults whose imagination and sense of connection to the world around them has been allowed to develop to its fullest potential. John Prebble, describing the Scottish Highlanders before they were cleared from the land 200 years ago, writes: "Their attachment to the land was deep and strong. They had peopled it with talking stones, snow-giants, and mythical warriors of mountain granite. Their culture was virile and immediate, their verse flowered on the rich mulching of their history".[5] Such are the links between land and culture that the loss of the former inevitably involves the erosion of the latter. Thompson remarks: "The commons and wastes shrank, in the nineteenth century, to the village greens (if such survived) and communally-shared custom shrank to the 'calendar customs' and survivals collected by the folklorists".[6]

Popular culture was also coming under deliberate attack. Traditional calendar customs as the Plough Monday procession were banned (in 1548), along with saints' days associated with special trades and occupations (1547). Keith Thomas attests: "By the dissolution of the religious gilds they put an end to such village institutions as plough gilds, hobby-horses and collections for plough lights. The annual feast of the parish church's dedication was compulsorily moved to the first Sunday in October, and all other wakes forbidden. Later ecclesiastical injunctions prohibited the entry into the church or churchyard of Rush-bearing processions, Lords of Misrule and Summer Lords and Ladies".[7] The same spirit continued into more recent times, reflecting the ruling classes' distaste for, or perhaps fear of, anything smacking of a sense of culture from below. Records local historian Chris Hare: "The Reform Bill of 1832 brought to power the new middle classes, who by temperament and conviction sought to 'civilise' society. Many old festivals with 'pagan' overtones were suppressed, and a professional Police force was established to clear the streets of the 'rabble' and ensure the protection of property".[8] Describing the state violence used to stamp down on any unauthorised expressions of collective cultural identity, he adds: "All over the country in the 1860s and 1870s, 'riotous' customs were being put down by force. At Guildford, between 1863 and 1865, the 'Guys', as the Bonfire Boys were known there, were brought to submission 'at the point of a bayonet' by troops specially drafted into the town".[9]

As we can see from the authorities' reaction to expressions of popular tradition, there are two ways of regarding the close relationship between a people and the land on which it lives, along with the culture that can prosper on that earthy bond. For someone who is determined to do away with the connection, and uproot the people from the land, it is convenient, and perhaps psychologically necessary, to regard it in purely negative terms. The same arrogant claims of racial and culture superiority used to justify the Empire were also trotted out by the British ruling elite as excuses for domestic land theft. Thus in a book published in 1824, John MacCulloch, Doctor of Medicine and Fellow of the Royal Society, was able to write of evicted Highland families in Sutherland and their love of their land: "The attachment of the wretched creatures in question was a habit; the habit of indolence and inexperience, the attachment of an animal little differing in feeling from his own horned animals... As children, it was the duty of their superiors to judge for them, and to compel them for their own advantage".[10]

The second way of viewing the land bond is to understand that it forms part of what Mircea Eliade calls our "feeling of mystical unity with the native Earth".[11] Eliade argues that this in fact goes far beyond an attachment to a particular native land and is "the mystical experience of autochthony, the profound feeling of having come from the soil, of having been born of Earth in the same way that the Earth, with her inexhaustible fecundity, gives birth to the rocks, rivers, trees and flowers. It is in this sense that autochthony should be understood: men feel that they are *people of the place*, and this is a feeling of cosmic relatedness deeper than that of familial and ancestral solidarity".[12] Heinmot Tooyalaket of the Nez Percés was expressing the same point of view when he declared: "The earth and myself are of one mind. The measure of the land and the measure of our bodies are the same".[13]

An important feature of this relatedness is that it emerges naturally, from below, and is not something imposed from above. The culture that is born from this sense of belonging has an inner strength and cohesion that it would be impossible to devise artificially. Individuals are united by a sense of common identity – with the land, with nature, with each other. Communities are held together in an organic fashion by what Thompson refers to as "an oral tradition, a customary consciousness, in which rights were asserted as 'ours' rather than mine or thine'".[14] There is no need, in this kind of society, for the codes and abstractions of Authority to create a false "order". As Peter Kropotkin observes: "For ages and ages mankind lived without any written law, even that graved in symbols upon the entrance stones of a temple. During that period, human relations were simply regulated by customs, habits and usages, made sacred by constant repetition, and acquired by each person in childhood, exactly as he learned how to obtain his food by hunting, cattle-rearing or agriculture".[15]

The idea of this organic society, this natural condition of mutual aid, of co-operative collective autonomy, is essential to Kropotkin's vision of anarchy. "Without social feelings and usages, life in common would have been absolutely impossible. It is not law which has established them; they are anterior to all law... They are spontaneously developed by the very nature of things, like those habits in animals which men call instinct".[16] In this view, human society should be a vital entity in which individuals are constantly interacting and co-operating like the organs within a human body.

Herbert Read develops this theory further by suggesting

that a living society of this kind must have a means of internal communication. He writes: "We are to be kept alive in more than one sense: first as individuals, then as communities, and finally as a species. To keep ourselves alive as individuals we must practise mutual aid – that is to say, we must form communities. It now begins to look as though, in order to keep alive as communities, we must practise mutual aid at the community level, and eventually as a species. In order to practise mutual aid, we must communicate with one another... the idea that words and symbols could be used positively, as synthetic structures that constitute effective modes of communication, does not seem to have occurred to our leading psychologists. Myth and ritual, poetry and drama, painting and sculpture – they have treated these creative achievements of mankind as so much grist for the analytical mill, but never as conceivably the disciplines by means of which mankind has kept itself mentally alert *and therefore* biologically vital".[17]

A bigger picture is progressively emerging here. The bond between humanity and land goes beyond the material to a psychological level, reinforced by customs, often directly related to that land. Together, this amounts to a culture. Part of the role of that culture, with all its tradition, myth, folklore, poetry and so on, is to ensure the cohesion and health of an organic community which has evolved in a co-operative and communal form in order to provide the mutual aid without which individuals cannot thrive. Culture therefore amounts more or less to the manifestation of a collective identity, a communal personality. This identity is not clear-cut and its edges must always necessarily be blurred and porous like those of the natural world from which it has arisen. It certainly shouldn't be confused with the artificial label of "identity" imposed on groups of people from the outside in order to encourage obedience and submission to an authority supposedly dedicated to protect the interests of the designated group. Indeed, this culture of autonomous collective identity is entirely incompatible with the system of Property, Law, Authority and State described in the last chapter: such is the fundamental difference between the two ways of understanding human life, moreover, that they must inevitably find themselves in constant conflict.

Thompson touches on this point when he describes the Highland Clearances as "testimony to the decisions of a law which afforded no shelter to a population evicted from lands which they had supposed to be communally owned, from time out of mind, by their clans. But the law could take no cognisance of such a communal personality".[18] If the law did not recognise the communal personality of a co-operative organic society, then that communal personality often did not recognise the law, either. The essential contradiction between the two outlooks cannot be overstated. Customs had evolved to protect and enhance the community. Law, although it may have included elements of custom as a kind of cover, was designed to protect an elite from that community. The result is a dislocation between, on the one hand, our innate sense of right and wrong and, on the other, the judgements of the law. This is still very much in evidence today, even if we sometimes put this down to a specific "miscarriage of justice" rather than the fact that the legal concept of justice is entirely alien to the natural one which lives on in our collective imagination. How often do we encounter a sense of disbelief that people who are obviously standing up for what they know is right can be treated as criminals by the judicial system and its violent enforcers?

That innate sense of authentic justice was the source of what Thompson labels the "legitimising notion" behind almost every crowd action in eighteenth-century England. He explains: "By the notion of legitimation I mean that the men and women in the crowd were informed by the belief that they were defending traditional rights or customs; and, in general, that they were supported by the wider consensus of the community".[19] The result of this was what he presents as the paradox of a *"rebellious* traditional culture", a popular culture which "is rebellious, but rebellious in defence of custom".[20] Bearing in mind the intrinsic conflict between the traditional communal personality and external authority, this phenomenon seems less paradox than inevitability! But since the term "tradition" has been co-opted and is perhaps now more generally associated with the mechanisms of repression than with the organic autonomy against which they are deployed, in contemporary Western terms Thompson's term is no doubt justified.

For a while, in any case, folk tradition went hand in hand with resistance to the encroachments of the new capitalist world order. Communal shaming rituals like rough music "were commonplace of industrial conflict, at least until the early nineteenth century", reports Thompson.[21] Uprisings in South Wales in the 1820s involved ritualistic elements, he adds: "men, with blackened faces, dressed as women; animal-guising, with horns, skins, and masks; the blowing of horns, lowing, rattling of chains, and firing of guns outside the homes of blacklegs or informers".[22] Twenty years later, in the same area, the "Rebecca Riots" were notable for their use of the *ceffyl pren* ("wooden horse") tradition and "Rebecca" itself was a term for an alternative folk justice, for an order from below. The theatricality and symbolism of the more radical kind of present-day protests, with their insistence that, for the moment at least, these are "our streets", are also surely a faded continuation of the same phenomenon.

All of these forms of defiance represent a threat to the status quo, though not necessarily in a strictly physical form. By presenting an alternative *conception* of tradition, of justice, of right and wrong, they challenge the *ideological* monopoly of the State. By presenting a community as essentially a collective personality, with the moral right to determine the shape of its own existence, they directly contradict the assumptions that the dominant forces want us unquestioningly to accept. The confrontational aspects of folk tradition only ever had to develop in the first place because of assaults on its values by the ruling classes: even without the element of resistance or protest, the mere *existence* of a communal entity born of custom, of a culture which arises from below and follows the demands of its own innate laws, is *unacceptable* to Authority.

Attacks on self-organisation, communal culture and collective identity have always been an extension of the original land theft and are very much part of the ongoing process of disempowerment. The prevalent system always targets anything which acts as a barrier to its control and exploitation of humankind. Writes Kropotkin: "We know well the means by which this association of lord, priest, merchant, judge, soldier, and king founded its domination. It was by the annihilation of all free unions: of village communities, guilds, trades unions, fraternities and medieval cities. It was by confiscating the land of the communes and the riches of the guilds. It was by the absolute and ferocious prohibition of all kinds of free agreement between men. It was by massacre, the wheel, the gibbet, the sword, and the fire that church and State established their domination and that they succeeded henceforth to reign over an incoherent agglomeration of 'subjects' who had no more direct union among themselves".[23]

Capitalism can only function if the mass of the population have no choice but to be part of its pyramid of exploitation. It cannot tolerate anyone opting out of its system and is always prepared to use violence to bring people under its economic control. This attitude shines through clearly in the words of James Loch, commissioner of the Stafford estates in Sutherland and thus one of the main architects of the Highland Clearances. He complained that the Highlanders were "contented with the poorest and most simple fare" and not interested in becoming part of the money-orientated capitalist economy. They were, he said, "accustomed to a roaming, unfettered life which attached them in the strongest manner to the habits and homes of their fathers, they deemed no new comfort worth the possessing which was to be acquired at the price of industry; no improvement worthy of adoption if it was to be obtained at the expense of sacrificing the customs or leaving the hovels of their ancestors". These attributes amounted to "formidable obstacles to the improvement of a people".[24] By "improvement" he meant the profits to be gained by the exploitation of the land, sadly impeded by the inhabitants' inconsiderate culture of non-materialist autonomy.

Journalist John Robertson, who reported on the Clearances for the *Glasgow National,* observed that "the Highlander's soul lives in the clan and family traditions of the past, the legends of the ingle, the songs of the bards" and that "the iron genius of economical improvements he knows not and heeds not".[25] Loch was quite explicit about the need to get rid of this authentic culture that was inconveniently holding back the progress of the money system, promising: "In a few years, the character of the whole of this population will be completely changed... The children of those who are removed from the hills will lose all recollection of the habits and customs of their fathers".[26] Prebble writes that Loch's policies "broke the spirit of a proud people"[27] and it is clear that this was a deliberate premeditated act, in the same way as in the course of several centuries in North America the spirit of many more proud peoples was deliberately broken when "several million Europeans and their descendants undertook to enforce their ways upon the people of the New World".[28]

As the European imperialists expanded their spheres of exploitation, it was the same story all over the globe, and countless "backwards" cultures with an "irrational" attachment to the land were wiped out in the name of Progress. On the other side of the planet from Scotland, in New Zealand, capitalism was faced with the obstacle of communally-owned land and so found it necessary to enforce what one Henry Sewell described as "the detribalization of the Natives – to destroy, if it were possible, the principle of communism which ran through the whole of their institutions... and which stood as a barrier in the way of all attempts to amalgamate the Native race into our own social and political system".[29] Culture, custom, co-operation, autonomy and connection to the land are all anathema to the capitalist system and it has always been prepared to use all its violence to eradicate them and stamp out the collective freedom that they enshrine.

III

UNDERGROUND FREEDOM

Just as the dominant system cannot tolerate any culture of autonomy which might threaten its hegemony, so it cannot allow the free expression of ideas beyond its control. They must therefore be repressed.

For many centuries this role of policing the possibilities of human thought was carried out in Europe by the Roman Catholic Church. Christianity had rapidly developed from its origins as a radical mystic cult to become the theological arm of the Roman Empire. Indeed, in this religious incarnation the Roman Empire could be said to have survived into the 21st century and accumulated a billion subjects, having expanded its sphere of influence beyond this continent to Central and South America (where, as the term "Latin America" informs us, the people today speak variants of the imperial language). An empire can only recognise one legitimate source of worldly power – its own – and likewise an imperial church can recognise only one truth, that being the one it imposes. Therefore, as Joseph Campbell remarks, "the outstanding feature of the Church's history in the West became the brutality and futility of its increasingly hysterical, finally unsuccessful, combats against heresy on every front".[1]

Any attempt to fully catalogue this ideological war would quickly become bogged down with detail, so many were its battles. By the fourth century, the Christian Roman Empire had already launched "a vast anti-pagan campaign across the whole of the Empire," writes Yves Delhoysie. "Pagan places of worship were demolished and country churches built in their place".[2] But at the same time as they attempted to neutralise the resistance of local folk tradition (*see also Chapter 4*), the Roman Christians were ironically carrying with them the seeds of different forms of "heresy". Campbell explains that a number of mystic faiths such as Mithraism and Gnosticism had been carried to northern Europe, along with official Christianity, by Roman colonization. "And there, following the victories of Constantine (324AD) and promulgation of the Theodosian Code (438AD) – which banned in the Roman Empire all beliefs and cults save the Christian – the mysteries, like a secret stream, went underground".[3] This, suggests Campbell, explains the origins of many of the heretical movements that lingered beneath the surface of "semi-Christianized Europe".[4]

The Romans' intolerance of other traditions within its Empire was ruthless and shocking: "Alexandria housed the greatest library of the ancient world until it was burnt down by the Romans in an act of vandalism worthy of Mao Tse Tung's red guards," writes Adrian G Gilbert.[5] The religious despots in Rome could not even tolerate unauthorised types of thinking within Christianity. The medieval Scholastic movement was crushed by the Church and its founder, Abelard, cruelly persecuted. In 1277 the Church issued a condemnation of no fewer than 219 unacceptable philosophical propositions, including the very thought "that there are falsehoods and errors in the Christian religion as in all others".[6] Later still, of course, the Church's claims to an absolute spiritual authority over the faithful were enforced by what Delhoysie calls the "police-state terrors of the Inquisition"[7] which rooted out the slightest sign of dissent or of a desire for intelligent discussion.

Linked to this religious hegemony was a worldly one. The Christian Church had realised that allegiance with Empire could serve its purposes and the rulers of Europe appreciated the role of an essentially submissive official creed in keeping the population in order. Occasionally, over the centuries, this Machiavellian approach has been openly voiced by the authorities, such as in 1698 when Lamoignon de Bâville, the administrator of Languedoc in southern France, was facing the prospect of a local uprising by religious dissidents (*see Chapter 5*). He wrote of the importance of religion in maintaining "the order of subordination and domination among men, which gives the weight of authority to some and bends the will of the others to obedience". On the other hand, he added, "when the subjects have a different religion to that of the prince, the domination of the latter cannot be complete, nor the dependence of the former".[8]

The crisis for the authorities was all the greater if the "different religion" involved – whether ostensibly part of Christianity or not – was not embedded with the same fundamental obedience to Authority that so marks the official Church doctrines developed under the guidance of the Roman emperors. At the core of this issue is the Christian insistence on a God completely apart from His creation, including humanity. This contrasts sharply with the old pantheistic conception of a divinity immanent in everything around us, in which people are essentially part of "God", however this is expressed, and are thus empowered to live according to the demands of the spirit within themselves, rather than the demands of an external authority claiming to represent the separate deity. Attempts to eradicate this holistic vision seemed doomed to failure. It kept finding new channels through which to reintroduce itself to the imagination of the peoples of Europe. Even after the soldiers of Rome had stopped inadvertently transporting such ideas around the continent, there were plenty of other routes by which the seeds of heresy could sneak in and reimplant themselves under the official topsoil of Christianity and keep sending up green shoots of spiritual freedom.

The Atlantic seaboard was one such entry point – we tend to forget in this age of motorways and high-speed railway lines that water was the main route of travel and communication in centuries past. There is evidence of a cultural spread from the Mediterranean and north Africa via the western coasts of the Iberian peninsular and Brittany to as far north as Ireland. Robert Graves, for one, speculates that certain non-Christian ways of thinking there "came from the East along with the complicated arabesques of medieval Irish illumination art and the curiously Persian or Arabian forms of ninth-century Irish poems".[9]

Islamic Spain was also an important influence, through the scholarship of its great cosmopolitan centres of learning. Further contact with the Arab world took place with the Crusades. As well as fighting against the Saracens, Europeans were frequently impressed by them and carried home with them certain of their ideas, which were then combined with their own pagan traditions to create new forms of an old freedom-based spirituality in fundamental conflict with authoritarian mainstream Christianity. An important role was played in this respect by the esoteric Islamic tradition of Sufism, which shares some of its origins with early Christian mysticism, including Gnosticism, and also with alchemy, which is, indeed, an Arab term.[10] Its ideas are also often close to the Hindu Vedānta. Opinions vary as to which Eastern tradition influenced which, but, as Idries Shah concludes, this debate "is of less importance to the Sufi than the fact that the mystical stream, its source, is essentially one".[11]

The Sufi influence on Europe is a neglected, but significant, one. The Gnostic faith, to which Sufism is so closely related, "reached as far as the medieval Cathars" and "underlies the hermetic cosmology that is the basis of Western occultism, running through alchemy to the hermeticism of the Renaissance",[12] according to Lynn Picknett and Clive Prince. They also point out that the Cathars, like the Sufis, were often

itinerant preachers, "living in the utmost poverty and simplic-
ity, stopping to help and to heal wherever they could".[13] Graves
describes the theme of love so often expressed by Sufis – "love
in the poetic sense of perfect devotion to a Muse"[14] – and adds:
"This love theme was later used in an ecstatic cult of the Virgin
Mary, who until the Crusades had occupied an unimportant
position in the Christian religion. Her greatest veneration
today is precisely in those parts of Europe that fell strongly
under Sufic influence".[15] He refers to the Saracen, probably
Sufi, origins of the troubadors[16] and detects Sufi traces
throughout European literature, from the legend of William
Tell to the tales of Don Quixote. The Knights Templar,[17]
Freemasonry,[18] and Rosicrucianism are all thought to have
been inspired by the Sufis, says Graves, and he concludes that
"Sufi thought continued to be a secret force running parallel to
orthodox Christianity".[19]

So what was the significance of this influence? Through the
distorting lens of Christianity, this hidden or "occult" stream is
something evil, to be feared. But in Sufi terms, the "Black Arts"
referred to wisdom rather than to Satan[20] and the tradition's
real threat consisted in the fact that "it follows a path other
than that which has been represented as the true one by
authoritarian and dogmatic organization",[21] as Shah observes.
This was the re-emergence in new forms of an important
current of spirituality repressed by Christianity, one which
offers the possibility of a direct personal experience of the
divine, without the need for intermediaries, and which leads to
all the radical implications of a profoundly anti-authoritarian
attitude. The Sufis helped Europeans rediscover the idea of
freedom, which the Church had attempted to wipe out. "All
Sufis are by definition equal and responsible only to themselves
for their own spiritual achievements",[22] writes Graves. They
injected this concept back into European culture in disguised
forms. The court fool, for example, with his "motley clothes,
cock crest, jingling bells, simple wisdom and utter disrespect of

authority is a Sufi figure",[23] he adds.

Georges Lapierre, exploring the rise of radical millenarianism in Europe, also finds a source in this same Sufi tradition. He reports: "In Spain, from the ninth to the twelfth century, various cities including Seville saw the activities of mystic Muslim fraternities, the Sufis or Holy Mendicants; once he had emerged from apprenticeship, during which he practised absolute obedience, the Sufi stepped out into a world of total liberty".[24] Their love of freedom spread far afield and can be seen throughout the diverse underground "occult" tradition in Europe, thus challenging the controlling and disempowering tenets of the Church. "Neither Gnostics nor hermeticists grovelled before their God," write Picknett and Prince. "Unlike Catholics, they did not think of themselves as lowly and evil creatures who were destined for purgatory, if not hell itself. Recognizing their divine spark automatically bestowed what we today would call 'self-esteem' or *confidence* – the magic ingredient in the process of fulfilling one's potential... the idea of mankind's essentially divine status did not accord with the Christian idea of 'original sin'".[25]

Whenever varieties of these interlinked Sufi-influenced "heresies" surfaced, they were attacked with the full force of the powerful Christian Church. The Albigensian Crusade in the first half of the 13th century saw 100,000 Cathars in Languedoc massacred on the orders of the Pope and it was specifically for the interrogation and extermination of the Cathars that the Inquisition was first created. At around the same time, a group of clerics at the University of Paris gathered around Amaury de Bène, who pursued a broadly pantheistic line by arguing that "God is the intelligence that organises and the essence of that which is organised".[26] He and his fellow thinkers were burnt at the stake in 1210, but over the next couple of centuries the movement they had sparked, known as the Brethren of the Free Spirit, spread all across the north of France, Belgium and Netherlands, Alsace, the Rhinelands, the south of Germany, Silesia and northern and central Italy.

The *Apostolici* who appeared in northern Italy at the end of the 13th century believed in communal life and the abolition of both private property and marriage and were inspired by Gherardo Segarelli. "He recognised neither leaders, hierarchies, churches nor religious ceremonies and urged his fellows to reject authority," relates Delhoysie. "Incarcerated several times, he fell into the hands of the Inquisition in 1287 and was burnt at the stake in 1300".[27] Two of his followers, Dolcino de Novare and Marguerite de Trente, were at the forefront of a 4,000-strong guerrilla army, which exploited its superior mobility to successfully strike against authority around Bologna, Modena, Milan and Como. Raoul Vaneigem explains how in 1305 they founded their own village in the mountains, where "a population of 1,400 people organised communally, in an atmosphere of liberty and solidarity".[28]

The growing Free Spirit movement was felt to be "the greatest threat that the authority of the Church had known up to then",[29] writes Delhoysie. Marguerite Porete, author of the influential *Mirouer des simples âmes* (*The Mirror of Simple Souls*) was executed in 1310 and in 1312 the Pope condemned all Free Spirit followers to the clutches of the Inquisition.

The tenor of the Church's objection to their ideas can be gauged by the contemporary comments of the cleric Jan van Ruysbroeck: "Thirsting for freedom, they want to obey nobody, not the Pope nor the bishop, nor the priest, and, however they might appear externally, they know no internal submission to anything, neither in their will nor in their works, for they are fully cut loose from all that belongs to the domain of the Holy Church".[30] The notion of "internal submission" was indeed alien to those who felt the divine essence within themselves. Vaneigem argues that the Brethren of the Free Spirit didn't so much reject religion as go beyond it. "God is denied in that since he is present in everyone, the moment you are conscious of that fact you have freed yourself from the shackles and the laws of spiritual and temporal power".[31] Lapierre emphasises that the Free Spirit's ideas presented a serious challenge to the church's self-appointed role as "necessary mediation between God and humankind".[32]

The repression continued, but the situation had now moved into a more advanced stage of conflict. Rather than let themselves be forced further underground, the new representatives of the old spiritual path were increasingly defiant, transforming their theoretical rejection of Authority into a revolutionary assault on power, property and privilege. Their ideas inspired both an uprising in Florence in 1378 and the Peasants' Revolt in the south of England in 1381, where a number of those involved had been linked with a previous outbreak of "heresy", including John Ball, who had been arrested for illegal preaching 20 years earlier. In 1418 a group of 50 people from Picardy in northern France, linked to the Free Spirit, turned up in Bohemia and joined forces with local rebels, known as Hussites after Jan Hus who had been burnt as a heretic in 1415.

At the same time as urban rebellion fomented in Prague, peasants around nearby Tabor came together to abolish private property and tax. They held all in common and called each other "brother". On 14 July 1420 a coalition of urban Hussites and rural Taborites routed the German troops who had been despatched to re-establish the control of the Emperor over Bohemia: "The union of the towns and the countryside had made it possible to crush the army sent by the Church and the Empire".[33] Revolts continued to break out periodically and in 1437 there were peasant uprisings in both Hungary and Romania, with another in Zbaszyn, Silesia, in 1440.

In 1476 a revolutionary messianic movement developed in the southern German village of Niklashausen. A young shepherd, Hans Böhm, had visions which he related to his family and then to the wider public: "He announced the Millennium, the return to primitive equality – authority and private property would disappear and all things would be held in common".[34] One day, he told the crowd to come back to the spot on the following Saturday, but this time armed and ready for action. The Holy Virgin would tell them what to do next. Böhm was taken away to Würzburg, where crowds of supporters tried to free him, but, with a certain historic inevitability, he was burnt at the stake.

Still the spirit of revolt could not be crushed. Before the end of the century a much more sophisticated secret revolutionary league called the Bundschuh had been set up in the towns of Alsace, uniting peasants with the urban poor plus a handful of bourgeoisie and minor nobles. Having gathered on a mountain in the Vosges and tried to start an uprising by taking Selestat, the survivors fled to Switzerland and southern Germany and re-established the organisation there. At the start of the 16th century there were further insurrections in what was then the Kingdom of Hungary, in which rebels demanded their "ancient rights"[35] and "castles and monasteries were destroyed everywhere and noble prisoners judged and executed by peasant juries".[36]

Here we clearly see the part played by repression in forging revolutionary attitudes. Even where the violence of Authority physically defeats rebellion, it has been forced to openly display that violence. Whatever the original causes of the revolt, they become merged with the defence of general freedom against this repression. The ruling system, for its part, becomes identified very strongly with the opposite principle, the *denial* of freedom. If Authority ignores the original signs of disobedience, it certainly risks losing the total control it always craves. But if it stamps down on them, this disobedience can harden into something that presents much more of a long-term challenge to its hegemony.

The only answer to this dilemma confronting Authority is that adopted by the advanced contemporary forms which rule us today. They have learnt to avoid creating a pre-revolutionary situation by pretending to respect freedom – in fact, by redefining "freedom" to describe their own systems of control. Through means we will discuss later, we have now reached the unhappy position where this deceit has been largely successful: the *very idea* of authentic freedom has been lost to our society, buried under layer upon layer of lie.

If this root concept of freedom, currently almost unthinkable, were ever once again to start spreading through the collective spirit, the authorities would not be able to tolerate its growth and would necessarily have to turn to the openly extreme repressive measures that they hold back as a desperate last resort. As an inevitable result, we would once again see collective psychological change such as that which took place at the end of the Middle Ages, when the abstract love of freedom innate to "heretic" spirituality was transformed, by the fires of repression, into a rebellion against the worldly power-system. Moreover, this rebellion carried within it a sense of purpose and momentum. In the hearts of the new generations of rebels, longing turned to desire, defence to attack. "They had stopped regarding the reign of liberty, equality and the total community as a distant Golden Age now lost for ever. They started to see it as an imminent possibility," writes Delhoysie. "The myth became a demand. Nostalgia for a happy and lost past turned into a dynamic dream of a near future which would restore this primal glory".[37]

IV

DISENCHANTED LIVES

At the same time as it was putting down threats of heresy and revolt across its empire, the Christian Church was still trying to consolidate its spiritual monopoly on an everyday local level.

While the physical separation of humanity from nature had been largely achieved with its displacement from the land, now regarded as Property rather than common birthright, there remained a strong emotional connection that had yet (and indeed *has* yet) to be completely severed. In nature, people and communities found a sense of identity and strength that was not drawn from above – from the institutional embrace of monarchy, Church, or State – but from below, from the earth itself. In nature they found the ancient gnarled roots of authenticity that exerted a much stronger pull on their inner loyalties than all the empty pomp that was supposed to confer an air of timeless legitimacy on the latest construct of fake Authority.

This deep-seated faith in the power of nature manifested itself in the folk tradition through beliefs and practices often collectively characterised as "magic", which could encompass anything from natural cures and faith healing through to alchemy, astrology or so-called witchcraft. The Church waged a long-term war against this tradition with the aim of gradually neutralising it. The initial stages were marked by what Keith

Thomas refers to as "the notorious readiness of the early Christian leaders to assimilate elements of the old paganism into their own religious practice, rather than pose too direct a conflict of loyalties in the minds of the new converts".[1]

Thus, rather than being completely destroyed – or, more probably, as the Church shrewdly realised, forced underground in a still-intact state – the old ways were, to adopt contemporary commercial jargon, *rebranded* as Christian traditions. Thomas explains that the ancient worship of wells, trees and stones was absorbed "by turning pagan sites into Christian ones and associating them with a saint rather than a heavenly divinity. The pagan festivals were similarly incorporated into the Church year".[2] While the population of Europe may have continued essentially to celebrate the old midwinter festival or midsummer's night, as long as they were ostensibly marking Christmas or St John's Day, the Church continued to feel that it was in control. What matter if the very name Easter, in English, had nothing to do with Christianity (deriving from the goddess *Eostre*) and that its date was still calculated in the old pagan manner, as the first Sunday after the first full moon following the vernal equinox, if it could be repackaged as a tribute to the death of Jesus Christ? Who cared if the widespread pre-Christian cult of the Mother Goddess bore little relation to the story of the Messiah? So long as its venerated statues of a maternal figure were not officially seen to be local pagan variations of Isis, the Christian Church was ultimately happy to embrace and own it.

However, the Christian hegemonists drew the line at anything that could be termed "magic". Much of this in fact amounts to the remaining vestiges of a very old human culture, with Thomas, for instance, comparing certain techniques of English "cunning" men and women with those of African diviners.[3] These healers and finders were the shamans and witch-doctors of their time and the demand for their services had not disappeared with the arrival of the various authorised modern representatives of religion or medicine. There was no room for them in Christian civilization and from its earliest years the Church had been trying to rid society of such "magicians". "By the thirteenth century," notes Thomas, "it had become customary for the clergy to pronounce an annual excommunication of all sorcerers *in genere*, and parish priests were expected to use the confessional as a means of coercing their flock into abandoning their time-honoured recourse to magic".[4]

The stern disapproval of the spiritual authorities was wide-ranging, with anyone from Welsh bards, Lollards or renegade priests facing punishment, often death, for any activity seen as tainted, including the issuing of prophecies. "In 1542 it was made a felony, i.e. a capital offence, to use magic for treasure-seeking, for the recovery of stolen goods or 'to provoke any person to unlawful love'", adds Thomas. "There were also numerous statutes against itinerant fortune-tellers, and a total prohibition of alchemy, the transmutation of metals remaining a felony until 1689. For most of the period, therefore, the main activities of the cunning men were blatantly illegal. Even the use of charms for healing was proscribed by the Church and banned by the various authorities responsible for licensing doctors".[5] A licensing system for midwives was brought in under Henry VIII (1509-1547), with oaths including a promise to refrain from the use of any kind of sorcery or enchantment during the period of labour. On top of all this, of course, came the campaign against "witchcraft" conducted all across Europe, which led to an estimated 1,000 witchcraft executions in England alone in the 16th, 17th and early 18th centuries.[6]

There was however, as anyone taking an objective view of the Christian religion will appreciate, a degree of hypocrisy in its stance against the broad range of "magical" thinking. The mysteries of the Church were not designed according to the demands of scientific rationalism and where could one honestly draw the line between the "superstition" of the heathens and the "faith" of the congregation, the rites of a witch or the ritual of a priest? From the Christian point of view, the situation was clear. The kind of magic carried out under its own auspices was heavenly in origin, while that carried out elsewhere was Satanic. It all came down to good and evil and the Church, of course, always represented the former. Others did not see it the same way. "Pagans had no horror of magic, for they did not associate it with the Devil", writes Colin Wilson. "Under Christianity, magic became Black Magic, and its power derived from demons, instead of from man's own hidden faculties".[7]

For the Church, the folk tradition of "magic" quite simply represented a challenge to its own authority, a rival source of spiritual power that prevented it from establishing the complete monopoly it been seeking since the far-off days of the newly-Christianized Roman Empire. This was why it had been happy enough to take on board so many pagan aspects during its conquest of European hearts and minds: its driving force was not a purity of faith but a *Realpolitik* intent on achieving domination on the temporal as well as the metaphysical plane. The power and the glory attributed to the Christian God was to be owned on Earth by those who declared themselves His sole representatives. While this necessarily meant stamping out religious rivals such as the Cathars or the Brethren of the Free Spirit, it also meant ensuring the population's allegiances were fully with the Church. As it was difficult to pinpoint and wipe out any specific sources of power within the tradition of "magic", the battle had to be fought on a more abstract level. Thus anyone representing *any* kind of alternative spirituality beyond the control of the Church, Catholic or Protestant, was either in league with the Devil or a charlatan.

The latter approach was taken with respect to the Hermetic writings which had inspired a mystical neoplatonism, a more contemporary kind of magic, as practised during the reign of Elizabeth I by the alchemist John Dee. A court scholar under James I, Isaac Casaubon, went to work to debunk the *Her-*

metica, ascribing to them a much later origin that had been supposed. This is still open to dispute, as it is notoriously difficult to be sure of the provenance of teachings that may have been copied and adapted many times, and indeed transmitted through the oral tradition. But, as Adrian G. Gilbert explains, there was an agenda behind Casaubon's state-endorsed research, published in 1614: "The study of Astrology, Cabbala and Spiritualism was all justified by reference to the writings of Hermes. Dismiss these as forgeries and the whole edifice of Renaissance Mysticism would come tumbling down, leaving the field clear for a re-emergence of pure, protestant Christianity".[8]

On a deeper level here we see in the battle against all forms of "magic" the re-enactment of a familiar struggle. The older traditions despised by the Church had arisen organically from human society and had not been imposed centrally from above. They thus represented nature and, by virtue of being an authentic expression of nature, they also represented the menace of freedom. This bid to disenchant nature was stepped up with the rise of protestantism, positivism and capitalism, as we will see. But it is worth pondering here whether all these centuries of repression have indeed "scrubbed the world clean of magic",[9] as Alan Watts claims.

On one level, attempts to wipe out the old ways have been an abject failure, as they live on in diverse forms today. For instance, a special dossier in the mainstream French newspaper *Le Figaro* in November 2013 reported on the continuing rise of neo-Druidism in that country and on the practices of 10,000 healers said to be active in France in the second decade of the 21st century.[10] Given the effort that Christianity has poured into wiping out such beliefs, this is pretty remarkable. As Thomas says: "The Church had all the resources of organized political power on its side, whereas most magical practices were harshly proscribed. The fact that they could still compete so effectively with the recipes of the established Church is testimony to their spontaneous basis in the needs of the people".[11]

However, on another level, the war against magic has been depressingly successful. The traditions that exist today are revivals of the original currents of folk belief. Like contemporary Morris dancing in England, they may look like the real thing, and may share many of its characteristics, but they are still essentially copies. René Guénon, writing in 1921, remarks that the solely oral transmission of many mystical, esoteric beliefs accounts "for the almost total disappearance of the doctrines of the Druids".[12] Their "reappearance" today is in fact the appearance of a new set of beliefs inspired by what is known of the original ones, though this is not to say that their presence in modern society is not welcome and the values they champion commendable – Liamme en Hengoun, for instance, told *Le Figaro* that "Druidism is neither a religion nor a philosophy, but a spirituality promoting harmony with nature".[13]

The problem lies not with those promoting these neopagan ideas, but with the context in which they are so doing. The original magic reflected the lives and practices of the population and this is no longer the case. Druids, Wiccans, healers and all others seeking to connect to the vital powers of nature unfortunately only add up to a small minority in the contemporary world and are sadly no longer a real expression of the living collective human soul.

Yes, there are still many human beings out there, among the billions populating the planet, who understand the bond between ourselves and the rest of nature and yearn to live the full potential that this offers us all. But, in the wealthier parts of the world at least, the majority of people seek gratification and purpose in life in the accumulation of material possessions, the seeking-out of novelty and the ephemeral and superficial mental stimulation offered by commercial entertainment. They embrace technology with enthusiasm, never question the need for the constant expansion of the industrial machine, submit themselves obediently to each new assault on their personal dignity, privacy, liberty. They often do not consider themselves qualified to question the detailed ways in which society is run, let alone address more fundamental issues of domination and authority. They may well profess belief in the religion they've been brought up to conform to, but it does little to inform their everyday lives, in which the overriding imperative will always be to "look out for number one". Nature is an occasional pleasant view from the car window and magic is a smug, slick besuited conman on the television screen. For them, and for contemporary human society taken as whole, the spirit is dead.

This isn't something that has just happened, or for which the population themselves can be blamed. It is the deliberate result of the disenchantment and disempowerment that has been inflicted on us for hundreds of years. We have been cut off from the sources which should provide our inspiration, even from the awareness that such inspiration *could exist*. As Thomas writes: "The acceptance of progress meant replacing faith in the wisdom of our ancestors by the conviction of their ignorance".[14] A belief in a timeless hidden potential inside each individual and inside each community is quite simply *dangerous* for the authorities. Once the magical possibilities of life are released from the genie's bottle there is no putting them back and that is why they must remain locked firmly inside the bank vaults, police stations, TV studios, council offices and church storerooms, securely in the hands of a power-friendly elite and well out of reach of the "general public".

V

FROM PROPHETS TO PROFITS

The suffocation of the human spirit has been a gradual process and there have been many moments in history where this has been openly resisted. One such instance came in the 16th century with the Reformation and the challenge to the domination of the Church laid down by what became the protestant movement. For a while it looked as if a real breakthrough might be taking place and that freedom would at last have the chance to shoot up through the cracks in the paving of power and burst into bloom.

The origins of protestantism can be traced back to a reaction against the repression meted out by the Church over the centuries, particularly during the peasant uprisings sketched out in Chapter 3. There was a general hatred of ecclesiastical Authority, which the rebel monk Martin Luther (1483-1546) seemed to incarnate when he took a stand against the might of Rome in the name of a Christianity stripped back to its basics. "He held up the Bible as the only basis for religion", writes Yves Delhoysie, "and with that the tradition and omnipotence of the Church were challenged".[1] The impression that protestantism offered a new hope seemed to be confirmed by the reaction from the Vatican, which regarded it as a dangerous heresy that had to be crushed.

Sadly, even by 1530, when protestantism made the final

break with the Vatican, there were clear indications that it was not the standard-bearer for human liberty that it had promised to be. But the switch-over, in much of northern Europe, from one form of religious authority to another had opened a breach in the lie of official "reality" – always the main barrier to authentic self-expression and self-determination – that could not immediately be closed and this vital pent-up revolutionary spirit continued to pour out into the world via protestantism for the next 200 years or so.

Throughout this outpouring, and in the various forms that this adopted, there are some interesting clues as to the origins of its blazing opposition to the established order, which make it clear that it is only by chance that it finds itself enmeshed with the ecclesiastical movement led by Luther, whose creed, as Ernst Bloch shows, "denies human freedom in all its possible forms".[2] In fact, the more closely one looks at the ideas expressed by the earlier protestant radicals, the harder it is to separate them from those previously voiced by the likes of the Brethren of the Free Spirit. And why should we try to separate them, anyway? The subtle forces behind the movement of history pay no heed to labels such as "The Reformation" and continue to transmit their often-invisible influence in the depths of the collective psyche of the *Zeitgeist,* regardless of all the surface activity around dates and personalities.

This influence was clearly at work in a man who began as a follower of Luther's. Thomas Münzer (1488-1525) was in fact recommended by Luther when he went out to preach in Zwickau in Saxony in 1520 – an endorsement that the prophet of Augsburg must afterwards have bitterly regretted. For when Münzer was thrown out of the town in 1521, and his supporters rioted in protest at his eviction, this was but the start of a massive European uprising against the very basis of Authority. Having escaped to Prague, postered a denunciation of the power of the princes in Mühlhausen, and sought brief refuge in Nuremberg, Münzer joined with Anabaptists – anti-authoritarian opponents of child baptism as a denial of free choice – to tour around Alsace, the Black Forest and Switzerland, stirring up revolt as they went.

From 1524, class war broke out all around Lake Constance, east to The Tyrol and Salzburg, west to Alsace and north to Franconia and Thuringia. Everywhere the people were rising up. 12,000 men under the blacksmith Ulrich Schmid in Ulm, 7,000 men in the Oberallgäu. Although these were termed peasant wars, the scope was much wider. Many towns were involved, and miners were notable among the ranks of the rebels. The 1525 insurrection at Mühlhausen saw the victorious population proclaim the communality of goods and the suppression of all authority. The revolt continued in Neckar, Odenwald, Franconia and Württemberg. The people overthrew the administration in Rothenburg, Pfullingen was taken by rebels, the townspeople of Stuttgart opened the gates to the peasants, insurgents attacked Würzburg and the bishop fled. Peasants around Strasbourg rose up and seized Ribeauvillé and Riquewihr in the Vosges. By mid-May the whole of Alsace was under the control of the insurgents and the French King felt forced to send in a 30,000-strong army to try and crush the rebellion.

Münzer was finally defeated at Frankenhausen in May 1525, then tortured and executed. But he had helped the people of much of Europe declare war on a new Establishment that had barely yet come into existence, with an effectiveness reflected by Luther's rabid condemnations of both him in person and the cause he represented. There can be no doubt that his struggle was the continuation of the peasant uprisings of the Late Middle Ages in a slightly different form – and in this he was truer to the original impetus behind the protestant revolt than was the authoritarian Luther. Georges Lapierre remarks that we see here exactly the same radicalism, characterised by "the rejection of private property, the holding in common of possessions, the total rejection of the institutions of state or religion, whether catholic or protestant".[3] Delhoysie traces this continuity back to Münzer's friend Nicklaus Storch, who had been deeply influenced by the thinking of the Free Spirit, and to the general ideas that were in the air at that place and at that time – "after all, Thuringia had been a bastion of heresy from the 13th to the 15th century".[4] Bloch, for his part, sees a clear connection between Münzer and "the old German mysticism" of Meister Eckhart, although these ideas had now been radicalised by an active millenarianism looking forward to a new heavenly age and the overturn of the established order.[5]

Given that Münzer and his comrades were the manifestations of a deeper current, it is hardly surprising that the movement didn't disappear with their defeat. The authorities, frightened by the spirit of revolt that been set free, persecuted the remaining Anabaptists, unleashing on them all the inhuman cruelty of the Inquisition. While some were thus eliminated, others were radicalised and in 1534, just nine years after Münzer's defeat, the northern German town of Münster rose up and declared itself the "new Jerusalem". "We have abandoned all which is contrary to our love of community and we would rather die than to return to the previous ways which, enslaved to egotism and property, lead to buying and selling, working for money, practising usury, eating and drinking the sweat of the poor", declared a text from the rebel city.[6]

It sent men to Strasbourg, Frisia and Holland to spread the word of revolt. Anabaptists organised in Maastricht and Aachen, while in May 1535 rebels came close to taking Amsterdam. Again, panic was sown among the authorities, with fears of uprising and invasions in France and Italy – it was said that the Anabaptists were preparing to march on Rome itself and there were rumours of sister uprisings in Spain and Turkey.

If this attempt to win freedom was again crushed by the overwhelming strength of worldly power, its flame had not yet died out. Anabaptists and their ideas spread further afield, across the Channel for instance, where they appeared in 16th century England among the Lollards and other sects. Christopher Hill explains that the Familists of Elizabethan England "were followers of Henry Niclaes, born in Münster in 1502, who taught that heaven and hell were to be found in this world"[7] and who was allegedly involved in the Münzer-inspired insurrection in Amsterdam. These Anabaptist ideas were carried across England by the likes of Christopher Vittels, an itinerant joiner of Dutch origin. "In the 1570s English Familists were noted to be wayfaring traders",[8] notes Hill. It would be wrong, of course, to imagine that the Münzer thread was the only way in which these ideas had reached England. They were direct descendants of the radicalism of the 1381 Peasants' Revolt, for instance. Lapierre also detects the posthumous influence of the author Marguerite Porete, who had been executed in 1310, commenting on "the astonishing success of the *Mirror of Simple Souls* in England from 1550 to 1650 and particularly among the Ranters whose theoretical and practical radicalism is close in every way to that of the Free Spirit movement of the late Middle Ages".[9]

An idea that is rooted in the authentic expression of human desire, and fuelled by a rightful rejection of injustice and tyranny, will find a thousand ways of reaching the consciousness of a new generation and will assume whatever external form most suits that particular age. Specific theories, whether religious or political, can provide a shape and form to what might otherwise remain deeply-felt but unarticulated urges and thus direct them towards a political revolt rather than into random individual acts of defiance or sporadic, localised outbreaks of anger.

The English Revolution may well seem to us, from our contemporary perspective, to have been a dead-end of Cromwellian despotism, or simply a historical stage in the rise of the noble and bourgeois classes at the expense of the monarchy, but at the time it would have felt like a lot more than that. Like the peasant uprisings in Germany, it came in the context of a general unpopularity of the religious establishment. Writes Hill: "In the late 1630s and 40s altar rails were pulled down, altars desecrated, statues on tombs destroyed, ecclesiastical documents burnt, pigs and horses baptized".[10] This was, as he says, a "period of glorious flux and intellectual excitement" when "literally everything seemed possible".[11]

The millenarianist sense of impending upheaval had already been stoked since 1618 by accounts of the bloody Thirty Years War on the continent and intensified by the dramatic sequence of events in England and Scotland – since relegated to the status of "civil war" rather than revolution by the British establishment – which led to the execution of Charles I in 1649, more than 140 years before the French carried out the very same constitutional reform. The principles that had inspired the German uprisings and had been spread by the Familists and the Lollards were thus ripe to be taken and adapted for this moment and combined with the particular ingredients and grievances of mid-17th century England. Peter Marshall describes the Diggers and Ranters of the English Revolution as representing "a hectic if short-lived revival of the 'Free Spirit",[12] but there was surely something even deeper resurfacing here.

Fifty years after the English Revolution another radical protestant rebellion broke out, this time in the Cévennes, in southern France, where protestants had been denied the right to public worship by the Roman Catholic state and, following years of repression, rose up in arms to proclaim their liberty. There was full-scale guerrilla warfare in the mountains, with churches burned, priests slaughtered and atrocities committed by both sides. For Bloch, the Camisard revolt which began in 1700 was the historical occasion on which Anabaptism clashed "for the last time with the firmly established and reinforced power of the sovereign state and its worldly-wise Church".[13]

The nature of the rebellion was, as one would expect, different again from that of Münzer or the Diggers. Nearly 200 years after the break from Rome, the protestantism of the Camisards was more formalised and Calvinist. However, as Bloch sees, there are "analogous phenomena and hopes" that bind it thematically with the early protestant revolts.[14] For a start, the religious content of the struggle was, like that of the German peasants and English radicals, combined with a hatred of authority that went deeper than their particular, justified, grievances. Gérard de Sède places the Camisard uprising within the context of hundreds of years of libertarian, egalitarian, Occitanian revolt against the central authority of the French state. Religious struggles such as these are, he concludes, "in the last instance only politico-social struggles waged on earth in the name of heaven".[15] And Philippe Joutard, in his history of the Camisards, comments that the millenarianism of the 16th century protestant radicals "had certainly disappeared from the preaching of the great 17th century intellectual men of cloth, but it lingered on in a latent state in the more humble of the faithful".[16]

There are other parallels which can be drawn between these superficially disparate uprisings which suggest they are in fact all manifestations – and not the only ones, to be sure – of what can be seen as fundamentally one social and spiritual phenomenon. Let us take, for instance, the matter of prophecies, which were prevalent and significant in all the uprisings we are discussing here. For Hill, this is a result of the protestant rejection of the traditional role of the Church as the sole means of communication between humanity and God: "The Reformation, for all its hostility to magic, had stimulated the spirit of prophecy. The abolition of the mediators, the stress on the individual conscience, left God speaking direct to his elect".[17]

Bloch, in his study of Münzer, describes him as "a believer fully aware that his superterrestrial mission depends on miracles and the strength of his mystical exaltation".[18] And Delhoysie relates how he used prophecy to fire up his army at the fateful battle of Frankenhausen by declaring that he would be unscathed by the enemy's cannon balls and lead them to a glorious victory: "He had to unleash in them a faith in the truth of their struggle, the self-confidence that alone can make you fit to fight. Nothing is impossible for faith".[19]

Here then is revealed the real power of prophecy – it is less a prediction than an attempt to *will* something to happen by declaring that it is *destined* to be. Not only are followers enthused and opponents demoralised by the *certainty* with which this is voiced (even though, in Münzer's and many other cases, this ultimately fails to materialise!), but there is also an attempt to force the hand of fate, to write history in advance, as you would like it to be written. A prophecy speaks not just of faith, but of determination. It expresses a sense of hope that is not content to remain abstract and passive but is harnessed to real desire and a commitment to physical action and courage, a hope that doesn't *depend on* physical contingencies but sets out to *shape and direct them* for its own ends.

There is always the risk that a prophet and his or her prophecies will appear ridiculous if the "prediction" fails to come true (which is obviously the case with contemporary cynical pseudo-prophecies, revolving around very specific dates for the end of the world, which are not under consideration here). But for a true prophet – expressing a genuine and positive desire arising from the collective unconscious – all restraint is cast aside in a single-minded resolve, rooted in the present moment, to set the course of the future. Credit is *borrowed* from the future to *gamble* on the present, with the conviction that if the attempt succeeds the cost will be more than repaid from the consequent spoils. And if it fails, well... so be it. When the stakes are so high it is no consolation in defeat to have spared oneself the embarrassment of looking ridiculous and, in fact, history usually looks back and sees tragic heroism in such failure, rather than absurdity.

Thus prophecies can often seem self-fulfilling, as Hill records of the English Revolution, when John Lilly's "repeated prophecies of a 'restraint on monarchical power', his call, on strictly astrological grounds, for Charles I and the Oxford Parliament to return to Westminster, his repeated predictions of defeat and a violent end for the king, may have contributed to bring about these effects".[20] He points out that astrological almanacs, with their ready source of authoritative-sounding predictions, sold even better than the Bible and "were alleged by many contemporaries to have done greater harm to the royal cause than anything else".[21] This was a time, writes Hill, when "ordinary people were freer from the authority of church and social superiors than they had ever been before, or were for a long time to be again"[22] and Keith Thomas says the fact that participation was not confined to the ruling classes "gave uncontrolled prophecy an anarchic character".[23] He adds that "the belief that God was on their side brought lower-class radicals self-confidence and revolutionary dynamism".[24]

In the Cévennes at the end of the 17th century there was a veritable epidemic of prophecies, as young people, termed *inspirés,* voiced their community's desire to break the chains of despotism. As ever, this was little understood by the flat minds of conformist society, with a Monsieur Brueys of nearby Montpellier formulating a medical theory to account for "a sickness of spirit or a kind of melancholic mania which leads those afflicted to believe they have the power to perform miracles and make prophecies".[25] One of these visions was experienced by Abraham Mazel, a 22 year old wool comber from St Jean du Gard, in an echo of the visions experienced by the young shepherd Hans Böhm in a different century, a different part of Europe and yet, somehow, the same human story. Mazel dreamt that there were some big fat black bullocks eating cabbages in the garden and he had to chase them off. The "spirit of the Lord" told him that the garden had represented the Church and that the bullocks were the priests who were devouring it. This was one of several *inspirations* which told him to gather men around him and take up arms against the Roman Catholic Church.

It was Mazel and the other young prophets, the *inspirés,* who restored joy and confidence to the movement, writes Joutard: "They also enabled craftsmen and peasants to overcome their sense of inferiority when up against the royal troops and thus to organise the longest-lasting popular insurrection against the *Ancien Régime* in France, one which provoked the greatest mobilisation of regular soldiers and made the strongest impression on Europe as a whole".[26] The enemy soldiers, without any strong conviction of their own, lived in fear of the Camisards' fervent renditions of battle-psalms, allowing the rebels to notch up some unlikely military victories, such as that at Alès in 1702 when Jean Cavalier and 60 other men saw off 700 state troops. The inner faith of the Camisards meant they were "on a roll" – going with the flow, or Tao. Their raids seemed to be aided by miracles and their confidence and courage soared. Recalled one guerrilla, Durand Fage: "Inspiration guided us in all we did. Death did not frighten us in the least".[27] Well might one opponent lament in 1702: "We haven't been able to put them down. They are desperate and furious men who'd sooner have their throats cut than surrender".[28]

Connected with the prophetic visions of the Camisards was a magical way of thinking owing little to the rigours of the protestant faith, which generally regarded any form of super-stition as evidence of "Popery". Joutard attests that the protestant peasants of the Cévennes "like all their compatriots in the working classes (Catholic or Protestant) were immersed in supernatural thinking on a daily basis".[29] The method they used to expose traitors and spies within their community is similar to that used by magicians, diviners or shamans in traditional societies anywhere in the world. Fage describes how in August 1703 a 30 year old *inspiré* called Clary declared at an assembly that there were traitors in their midst: "Clary, still in his ecstasy, got up and walked, sobbing and eyes closed, jerking his head and holding his clasped hands in the air. In this state, he went up to the traitor who was in the midst of the assembly and laid his hand on him".[30] These convulsions and tremblings were the only language left for people who could no longer express themselves in rational terms because of the way their culture had been brutally repressed, argues Joutard. They used "the only kind of speech that was left to them, that of their body. And those watching understood this language perfectly, because it coincided with the traditional means of expression of peasant culture".[31]

The same influence of the folk tradition can be seen in England, where magical thinking also played a part in protestant society, filling a gap in spiritual authority opened up by the Reformation. "It is true that in the long run protestantism worked against all magic, black or white, against charms, spells, incantations and love potions," comments Hill. "But it was a long time before these things affected ordinary men and women. Meanwhile, cunning men took over many of the jobs previously performed by Roman Catholic priests and neglected by their successors".[32]

In the sixteenth and early seventeenth centuries the cult of magic existed alongside protestantism, adds Hill, and "astrology, alchemy and natural magic contributed, together with Biblical prophecy, to the radical outlook".[33] Alchemy – an esoteric path imported, as we have seen, from the Muslim world – was recognised by Familists and other precursors of the Ranters and Quakers as "an outward symbol of internal regeneration"[34] in a melting pot of spiritual ideas inconceivable to our own pragmatic age. English revolutionaries were influenced by Italian neoplatonists and German Anabaptists[35] as well as the work of Francis Bacon (1561-1626), an early protestant philosopher influenced, as Isaac Newton was to be, by alchemical notions.

Münzer and the Anabaptists were fond of quoting Plato. Bloch, judging their uprising as "the most spiritual revolution that the world had known up to that point",[36] sees it as drawing on ancient roots and representing essentially "the breaking out and the expansion of the old heretic movement".[37] His instinct is confirmed by a comparison with the Cathars of the 12th and 13th centuries, for instance, who shared many of the attitudes of the later protestant radicals in the south of France, and indeed elsewhere: "Their way of life was an attempt to obey the teachings of Jesus. They accused the Catholic Church of having diverged much too far from the original concept of the Jesus movement. They regarded as anathema the wealth and pomp of the Church, which they saw as being the opposite of what Jesus had intended for his followers... Cathars led very simple lives. They preferred to meet in the open air or in ordinary houses rather than in churches, and although they had an administrative hierarchy that included bishops, all baptized members were spiritually equal and regarded as priests".[38]

This is not to say that their faith was the same as protestantism, because it wasn't, but underneath the period costume of the respective theological positions we see the same basic body of thought. Behind the radicalism of the early protestant movement in fact lies something which is not really Christianity at all, but an ancient spirituality that might best be termed a kind of pantheism, a belief in the oneness of a living cosmos. Take, for instance, the *Divine Teachings* of the clergyman-turned-Ranter Richard Coppin, published in 1649. He writes: "God is all in one, and so is in everyone. The same all which is in me, is in thee; the same God which dwells in one dwells in another, even in all; and in the same fullness as he is in one, he is in everyone".[39] Another Ranter, Leicestershire shoemaker Jacob Bauthumley, declares that all creatures of the world "are but one entire being",[40] adding that God is in everyone and every living thing: "man and beast, fish and fowl, and every green thing, from the highest cedar to the ivy on the wall".[41]

Gerrard Winstanley, spokesman for The Diggers, writes in *The Law of Freedom* that "to know the secrets of nature is to know the works of God". Showing an obvious influence from sources beyond Christianity, he continues: "And indeed if you would know spiritual things, it is to know how the spirit or power of wisdom and life, causing motion or growth, dwells within and governs both the several bodies of the stars and planets in the heavens above; and the several bodies of the earth below, as grass, plants, fishes, beasts, birds and mankind. For to reach God beyond the creation, or to know what he will be to a man after the man is dead, if any otherwise than to scatter him into his essences of fire, water, earth and air of which he is compounded, is a knowledge beyond the line or capacity of man to attain to while he lives in his compounded body".[42]

There had been a similar undercurrent to the earlier radical movement in northern Europe, with Bloch referring to the "esoteric" nature of Münzer's beliefs.[43] For the Anabaptists, says Lapierre, "spirit is what is universal in man, while egotism and greed are what separate man from his essence".[44] This is the same conviction that we saw in the Brethren of the Free Spirit and the Sufi tradition from which they drew their inspiration. The only label that the Ranters in England seem to have accepted was that of "my one flesh"[45] – a direct reference to this root idea that God is in everything and that we as individuals are merely temporary physical manifestations of that divinity.

There are two very strong philosophical, and political, positions that necessarily follow from such a belief. Firstly, there is, as Hill sets out, "a denial of the dualism which separates God aloft in heaven from sinful men on earth".[46] Secondly, there is recognition of an equality inherent within humankind, and indeed all living creatures. We are all of the one flesh, we are all brothers and sisters united in our common identity with God. These two beliefs converge into an absolute rejection of Authority in all its forms. There is no separate and remote God to give us orders. There are no intermediaries who can present us with texts or laws that we should obey. The spirit of God is in all of us and thus we obey our own hearts, our own consciences. No living creature is any more special than any other, so there is no reason for us to take orders from anyone or to respect their claims to have the right to wield power over us, whether in the name of temporal or spiritual authority. The crippling and disempowering Christian notion of "original sin" is also thus rejected and indeed pretty much reversed.

Here, already, we have a powerful revolutionary stance – a belief in complete freedom and complete equality. Not for nothing are the ideas of the Free Spirit or the Diggers often cited as early examples of anarchism.[47] When the potential of these beliefs is combined with the millenarianist factor – the belief that the established order is about to, and *should* be about to, fall and that the arrival of a new age is imminent – we also have a sense of urgency and direction that leads to action. In the language of the anarchist Gustav Landauer, the *Geist* of an egalitarian, non-dualist, anti-authoritarian spirituality is mixed with the *Wahn* of "a sense and purpose of life and the world",[48] thus creating a revolutionary movement with a power of conviction and a forward-moving momentum. This, perhaps, is the relevance of the Old Testament so much quoted by the Anabaptists, the Camisards and the English revolutionaries – it enhances the radical mix with the messianiac Jewish belief in the coming of the Messiah at a real time in the historical future, rather than the more abstract Christian love of a Messiah who has already been and gone, on the historical level, but lives on in a timeless dimension.

From the vantage point of the 21st century, religious belief often appears as an impediment to genuine radicalism. We tend to look back at the past and see movements or ideas as being revolutionary *in spite of* their religious content rather than *because of* it – but in the context of this earlier period we plainly have it the wrong way round. It was the spirituality of these radicals, in both passive (*Geist*) and active (*Wahn*) forms, that informed, firstly, their political beliefs and, secondly, their commitment to do something about them. Thus it was that when Winstanley rejected private property, it was on the basis that it was "antichristian, embodied in covetousness or self-love"[49]– a moral stance echoed two centuries later in the Christian anarchism of Leo Tolstoy.

With the benefit of hindsight, the English Revolution – like the peasant uprisings in northern Europe and the Camisard revolt – looks like a brief interruption of the course of history, rather than a turning point. Hill comments that before the upsurge of radicalism "the gentry and merchants who had supported the Parliamentary cause in the civil war expected to reconstruct the institutions of society as they wished, to impose their values. If they had not been impeded in this, England might have passed straight to something like the political settlement of 1688 – Parliamentary sovereignty, limited monarchy, imperialist foreign policy, a world safe for businessmen to make profits in".[50] In 1660, when England restored the monarchy and more or less returned to this anticipated path towards bourgeois Progress, there was an inevitable backlash against the ideas that had so threatened the status quo. "After the Restoration religious enthusiasm and levelling were bracketed together in the minds of the ruling classes," states Thomas "and they did not tire of insisting that the voice of the people should never again be confused with the voice of God".[51]

The flames of religious radicalism were not completely extinguished, of course, and their embers continued to glow. George Fox and the Quaker movement kept many of these ideas alive. Gerald Bullett writes that Fox repudiated in seventeenth-century protestantism both "bibliolatry, the fetishistic worship of the Old and New Testaments, and that doctrine of total human depravity which implies the utter separation of man from God. Against these traditional tenets of protestantism he affirmed the inwardness of authority and the presence of God in every human soul".[52]

A century later came William Blake (1757-1827), who, according to Hill, "owed much to the radicals of the seventeenth century"[53] – a view shared by A.L. Morton among others. Marshall describes Blake as the product of "a radical libertarian Protestantism" which had "produced some of the greatest thinkers of the day: Thomas Paine, Richard Price, Joseph Priestley and William Godwin".[54] He detects an inspiration for Blake's Romantic vision in "an underground heretical tradition which influenced his thought in a communitarian and chiliastic direction".[55] Passed down by the "mystical anarchists" of the millenarian sects of the Middle Ages, especially the Brethren of the Free Spirit, via the English Revolution, this lived on in Blake's day in sects like the Muggletonians and Taskites.[56]

But Blake was a voice of resistance to the age in which he lived, rather than a representative of its spirit, and by then mainstream protestantism in England showed little sign of any radicalism and had become as closely associated with Authority as the Church of Rome from which it had split. It would be satisfying to argue that the spirit of protestantism had thus been betrayed, but although it "began by looking like a great liberation of the human spirit",[57] the tone of its true nature had been instilled in it right from the start through the personality of its founder.

Luther, whom Bloch credits with an "authoritarian instinct",[58] was very quick to combine his rejection of the authority of Rome with an enthusiastic acceptance of the authority of the German princes. He condemned the uprisings of 1525 and indeed called for them to be violently crushed. He argued that the injustice and wrong deeds of authority did not justify revolt. It wasn't the place of ordinary men and women to punish wrong-doers – this was the sole prerogative of those in power. Luther's version of Christianity demanded patience and pacifism, insisting that it would be profaning the name of Christ to use violence in his name. He branded Münzer a "murderer" in 1525 and the following year his flunkey Phillip Melanchton wrote a *History of Thomas Münzer* in which he declared that the rebel leader had been possessed by the devil and dreamt up a "false and seditious doctrine".[59] Bloch sees the Caesarist mentality of Luther and his followers as tying in with a preference for the New Testament over the Old Testament which was so beloved of the messianic revolutionaries.[60] This would, ironically, mean that the man who led the revolt against the Roman church was foremost in promoting elements of obedience to authority which the Romans had emphasised and exploited to bolster imperial rule! Landauer also condemns Luther in his 1907 work *Revolution*, saying that he "radically separated life from faith and substituted organized violence for spirit".[61]

In any case, by 1525 we can already see protestantism as we know it today: craven in its obedience to worldly authority and eager to promote submission and slavery in the name of Christian pacifism – dismissed by Bloch as a "fake goodness" designed to lull people into compliance with a "dictatorship of injustice".[62] Its collaboration with earthly power can be seen again and again through history, such as during the Highland Clearances in 1830 when one Rev. Alexander Macbean rode around Strath Oykel advising people to surrender to the Writs of Removal issued by the land thieves. Faced with an initial refusal, he used the full psychological force of his religion to impose the desires of the landowners on the inhabitants, with John Prebble noting that "it took Mr Macbean another forty-eight hours, during which he described for them the fires of Hell, before their will broke".[63]

Together with this hatred of freedom – perhaps, in fact, as another aspect of it – came a flatness and dullness that still typifies the protestant creed, a complete lack of the timeless sense of inspiration that motivated the radical movements fighting under its banner. Writes Delhoysie: "Luther reduced life to its prosaic parts and ruled out any spiritual energy, any initiative to rise up above the day-to-day".[64] This profoundly unspiritual, in fact anti-spiritual, mindset formed part of the protestant psyche from the start and even partly informed their criticism of the Roman Catholic church.

Protestants correctly identified most Catholic rites as "thinly concealed mutations of earlier pagan ceremonies"[65] and, rejecting this co-option of older traditions, tried to root out all traces of anything not directly part of the Christian creed. Recounts Thomas: "Much energy was spent in demonstrating that holy water was the Roman *aqua lustralis*, that wakes were the *Bacchanalia*, Shrove Tuesday celebrations *Saturnalia*, Rogation processions *ambarvalia*, and so forth".[66] The result was an often-violent attack on what was left of the folk religions in Christian times, as Rupert Sheldrake describes: "Images of the Holy Mother and of saints and angels were broken and burned; stained glass windows were smashed; holy wells and wayside shrines were defiled; the tombs of saints broken open and their relics scattered; pilgrimages suppressed; many of the customary rituals and ceremonies abolished".[67] For all their spiritual motivation, the Anabaptists of Münster were also affected by an anti-cultural mania, destroying manuscripts and musical instruments in their "puritanical iconoclasm".[68] The protestant communities of the Cévennes had, even before the uprisings, taken it upon themselves to wipe out any elements of folk culture that they associated with paganism, such as bonfire nights, charivari (the French form of rough music) and all the saints' festivals and dances[69] and the Camisards maintained that hostility.[70]

These were ominous signs of the way that protestantism was to develop, cutting off human beings from the spiritual connections to the natural world which had lived on in such traditions and leaving them alone and unrooted, miserable sinners fit only to offer submission to a remote God and to the worldly powers whom he ordered them to obey. "All traces of magic, holiness and spiritual power were to be removed from the realm of nature",[71] as Sheldrake observes, and in this way the protestant Reformation perfectly prepared the philosophical ground for the mechanistic thinking that came to dominate from the 17th century. "Nature was already disenchanted and the material world separated from the life of the spirit; the idea that the universe was merely a vast machine fitted well with this kind of theology".[72]

This disenchantment of the world went hand in hand with a general narrowing-down of the mind. Says Hill: "After 1660 everything connected with the political radicals had to be rejected, including 'enthusiasm', prophecy, astrology as a rival system of explanation to Christianity, alchemy and chemical medicine".[73] As a result the connections between these ideas became somewhat lost. Religion largely ceased to be associated with revolution, while alchemy, prophecy and astrology were increasingly regarded as outmoded and irrelevant ways of thinking, even if a debased form of the latter continues to attract the popular mind to this day.

"Many babies went out with the bath water as the Royal Society trumpeted its respectability and concentrated on utilitarian experiments," writes Hill. "The wide vision, especially the social vision, of the radical Baconians was totally lost; some glimpses only survived in the Dissenting Academies. For the nonconformist sects, as they abandoned hope of turning the world upside down, as they readmitted sin, accepted existing society and the state, withdrew from politics to an exclusively other-worldly religion – so they lost their sympathy for and understanding of the earthly aspirations of Hermetic philosophy, of magic".[74] The alchemists and hermeticists of the previous age – John Dee, Giordano Bruno, Robert Fludd and others – had wanted to understand the universe as a whole and this thirst for holistic knowledge was reflected in the radical aspirations of Winstanley, who wanted science, philosophy and politics to be taught in every parish by elected non-specialists: "He and the radical scientists wanted science to be applied to the problems of human life: this was the practical significance of their emphasis on astrology, alchemy and natural magic. Their defeat, however scientifically necessary and desirable, also meant the end of dreams of an all-embracing *Weltanschauung* [world view] accessible to ordinary people".[75]

As polymaths made way for specialists and dreams made way for facts, utilitarian protestantism helped pave the way for a pragmatic and unimaginative new world. Following the Camisard uprising, that last hurrah of spiritual radical protestantism, people were, says Bloch, to increasingly adapt and conform to the established order: "From now on there will only be room for man such as he is, for *homo œconomicus*, and not for the true man guided by spirit, *homo spiritualis*".[76] From its earliest days, protestantism was linked to the rise of the bourgeoisie and this class's desire to embark on economic expansion without restraint and competition from the Roman Catholic Church and feudal society. De Sède notes that early Calvinism was more common among the middle classes than amongst the nobles and was mostly found in areas, such as Languedoc, "where the industrial, commercial and banking bourgeoisie was firmly ensconced".[77] The people of the Middle Ages, and their religion, had felt a profound distaste for money and the affront to their own values that it represented. The protestant work ethic, of which wealth was the natural consequence, "put an end to the guilty conscience experienced by Christians of the Middle Ages when dealing with money",[78] says Delhoysie. By bringing about the "reconciliation of commerce and faith",[79] he argues, protestantism even amounts to "a theological justification for money".[80]

Certainly, over the centuries, protestants have continued to feel that there is no real clash of principle between their religion and their pursuit of money, with the proviso, perhaps, that their business is conducted along supposedly "ethical" lines. A good example of this tradition can be found in Saltaire, near Bradford in northern England, where a non-conformist protestant church takes pride of place in the way that a cathedral would traditionally have done. This English town was founded in 1851 by protestant industrialist Sir Titus Salt to serve his textile business. The official line is that Salt was a philanthropist, moving his workers and their families out of slum conditions in Bradford to beautiful healthy surrounds. However, they now all lived in the shadow of a massive new factory in a purpose-built town (named after their humble Christian employer) which was conveniently close to a canal and railway and contained no inns or taverns to distract the workforce from their true vocation in life – making money for Titus Salt! Even the Quakers, those survivors of radical protestantism, have managed to combine the ethical sense that feeds their defiant pacifism with a taste for founding business dynasties – these include not just chocolate-makers Cadbury's, Terry's, Fry's and Rowntree but also shoe manufacturers Clarks and the Lloyds and Barclays banking empires.

Hill says two different revolutions took place in England in the 17th century. The radical one of the Diggers and Ranters failed. But the other revolution, which did succeed, "removed all impediments to the triumph of the ideology of the men of property".[81] And for Bloch the protestant Reformation can even be said to have introduced the elements of an entirely new faith – "that of capitalism, now elevated to the status of religion and become the Church of Mammon".[82]

The high priests of capitalism like to tell their worshippers that theirs is a religion of freedom and indeed they do feel compelled to challenge the powers of the state when their own money-making exploits risk being restrained. However, the truth is that capitalism is totally dependent on the machineries of the state, its laws and its enforcement processes, to maintain the population in the requisite state of servility. The unquestioning obedience to Authority prescribed by Luther is thus another useful contribution made by protestantism to the capitalist cause.

The symbiosis doesn't end there: the protestant rejection of the pantheist tradition also played into the hands of the exploiters who today control the world. For those who possess a holistic spirituality, the Earth is bountiful. Life is all around us and is also within us, and moves in natural cycles. We are born, we live and we die. If we plant seeds, they grow. All we have to do is "go with the flow", to revisit this Taoist term, respect nature and play our small part in the Whole. For any Christian, but particularly a Protestant, things don't just happen on their own. A supreme ruler is making it all happen and is controlling it all, every inch of the way. "All post-Reformation theologians taught that nothing could happen in this world without God's permission",[83] as Thomas states. Authority, from above, is therefore set in direct opposition to freedom from below. God, and the principle of Good, is associated with Authority while the Devil, and the principle of Evil, is associated with its opposite, the anarchy of unregulated and organic freedom.

Here we can see the deeper reasons behind the intense distrust of nature felt by protestantism and by its secular philosophical successors. For them, there is no divinity – and thus no innate goodness – in nature, in life or in humankind. This is all very convenient for capitalism. A disenchanted world is one which can readily be converted into money, the only true god. It's almost as if protestantism was sent in as an advance party to clear away any obstacles to the final victory of the forces of Profit. No sentimental attachment to old ways, or places, could be allowed to get in the way of the new creed of material expansion.

If an ancient wood was no longer inhabited by the spirits of the forest, there was nothing to stop it being chopped down and the timber used to provide a very solid lining to somebody's pocket. If a holy well was no longer holy, because that smacked of "Popery" or devilish paganism, there was nothing to stop its water being used by the machineries of industrialisation. If the earth was no longer the Mother, then there was no social taboo against ripping open her belly and tearing out her innards to convert them into steam and gold. God had provided animals and the land for His people to dominate and exploit as they saw fit – there were therefore no moral barriers to Progress.

It wasn't just nature that was "disenchanted" in a brave new world as stark and stripped-down as the inside of a Protestant church – with no place for notions of magic or mystery – but life itself. The hostility to pantheism, to any idea of an innate common vitality uniting all things, was transformed into a dogma. For Thomas Hobbes (1588-1679), whose philosophy Hill describes as "a secularized version of the protestant ethic",[84] humanity was brutal and selfish. Individuals were not part of an organic collectivity and naturally predisposed to co-operation, but would fight among themselves if left to their own devices – Authority was therefore absolutely essential to create some sort of order from above. John Locke (1632-1704) took this a step further by insisting we possess no innate sense at all. We are born with minds like white paper, void of all characters, without any ideas. Freedom from below, sourced from this nothingness, is therefore unthinkable.

Nature, spirit and freedom are all denied by this flattest of all philosophies, the materialistic mechanistic positivism justifying the monstrous rise of industrial capitalism under the protection of the State. The role played by protestantism in this disastrous shift in attitudes is a matter of record. Hill, for instance, remarks that "English and Scottish Presbyterians anticipated Hobbes in teaching that it was the function of civil government to restrain the depravity natural to all men",[85] while Delhoysie concludes that "protestantism paved the way from the Church to the modern State"[86] – a view also shared by

Landauer.[87]

It seems that members of the political establishment were also aware of the connection. René Guénon writes of the imperialist British state's attempted use of the protestant mindset to control the population of India, where an obstructive old-fashioned belief in the unity of all things had not been wiped out in the way it had been back in Blighty. He describes how in the first half of the 19th century, Rām Mohun Roy founded the Brahma-Samāj or "Hindu Reformed Church", complete with protestant-style services, at the behest of Anglican missionaries. Says Guénon: "It marked in fact a first attempt to convert Brāhmanism into a religion in the Western sense, and at the same time it showed that its promoters wished to make of their venture a religion animated by the self-same tendencies that characterise Protestantism. As was to be expected, this 'reforming' movement was warmly encouraged and supported by the British government and by British missionary societies in India; but it was too openly anti-traditional and too flatly opposed to the Hindu spirit to succeed, and people plainly took it for what it really was, an instrument of foreign domination".[88]

VI

CREATIVE BLOCK

Although the spiritual self-realisation of both individual and community was often blocked by the monopolistic fervour of Church and State, there had always been alternative channels through which it could find expression.

Within the cathedrals that ostensibly paid tribute to Authority, for instance, there sprouted glorious flowerings of the creative human spirit shaped by the rich imaginations and expert hands of skilled craftsmen. To gaze upon the work of medieval masons is to forget that there ever could be a line dividing manual craft from the more abstract notion of art: this distinction seems to be an invention of modern, specifically Western, civilization.

Ananada K. Coomaraswamy explains that in India "literature provides us with numerous lists of the eighteen or more professional arts (*śilpa*) and the sixty-four avocational arts (*kalā*); and these embrace every kind of skilled activity, from music, painting, and weaving to horsemanship, cookery, and the practice of magic, without distinction of rank, all being equally of angelic origin".[1] Herbert Read praises the Ancient Greek respect for craftsmanship, which included the fundamental conviction that "there is an inherent rightness in the exercise of a craft"[2] and muses: "A society in which every man would be an artist of some sort would necessarily be a society united in concrete creative enterprises: in a single creative enterprise, because in such a society the arts are unified".[3]

In this dream of what once was and what could be again, he echoes William Morris's evocation of times "when the mystery and wonder of handicrafts were well acknowledged by the world, when imagination and fancy mingled with all things made by man; and in those days all handicraftsmen were *artists*, as we should now call them".[4] In the light of this nostalgia, it is clear that by the second half of the 19th century, in which Morris was writing, this happy state of affairs had already disappeared. By then, the idea of creative craftsmanship had been reduced to that of functional production, following the requirements of, in Morris's words, "what is called Commerce but which should be called greed of money".[5]

For those who worship only money, the presence of beauty in any item is necessary solely to increase saleability. Any idea of inner value, unrelated to price, has no place on their balance sheet. Why would a cobbler trouble to spend long hours producing the best shoes of which he was capable, if he could knock out five pairs in the same time and still get away with charging the same price for what is, after all, a necessary purchase? Why would a builder use the finest materials and weigh up carefully what designs would sit most sympathetically with the surrounds, if the cheapest brick box would serve the same purpose and increase his profit? What matter if any of these end products lack quality? So long as they still make money they are fulfilling their role in a society where quantity reigns.

The effect of this change on the men and women who once practised crafts is dehumanising and humiliating. The machines that facilitate the speeding-up and skilling-down of manufacture are said to save "labour", but that is only true from the selfish perspective of the exploiter who resents the impact on his profit margins of the necessity of paying a decent wage to those who create his wealth for him. As Morris points out: "What they really do is to reduce the skilled labourer to the ranks of the unskilled, to increase the number of the 'reserve army of labour'– that is, to increase the precariousness of life among the workers and to intensify the labour of those who serve the machines (as slaves their masters)".[6]

Today this arrangement has become so familiar to us that it is taken for granted and rarely challenged, but as it was introduced and intensified it did provoke the wide criticism it surely merits. Artur Holitscher, for instance, writes in 1912 that "the specialisation of labour arising from mass production is increasingly reducing the worker to the level of a dead piece of machinery, a cog or lever functioning with automatic precision".[7] Franz Kafka, ever-sensitive to the fate of the degraded individual, condemns as "sacrilege" the system of mass-production known as "Taylorism", declaring in an interview: "The noblest and most unfathomable part of the whole of creation – time – is trapped in the snare of impure commercial interests. These conditions sully and debase not only creation but even more so the people who form part of it. A Taylorised life of that kind is a terrible curse from which can only result hunger and misery instead of the wealth and benefit that is desired".[8]

The conversion of craft into mass production led to its separation from the sphere of art to which it naturally belongs and thus alongside the relegation of the craftsman to slave status came the divorce of the artist from both people and culture. "The artist came out from the handicraftsmen, and left them without hope of elevation, while he himself was left without the help of intelligent, industrious sympathy," says Morris. "Both have suffered; the artist no less than the workman".[9]

Coomaraswamy also notes that in industrial society "in place of vocation as the general type of activity we find the types of individual genius on the one hand, and that of un-skilled labour on the other"[10] and concludes that what has been introduced is effectively a "spiritual caste system".[11] He explains: "Those who have lost most by this are the artists, professionally speaking, on the one hand, and laymen generally on the other. The artist (meaning such as would still be so called) loses by his isolation and corresponding pride, and by the emasculation of his art, no longer conceived as intellectual, but only as emotional in motivation and significance; the workman (to whom the name of artist is now denied) loses in that he is not called, but forced to labor unintelligently, goods being valued above men".[12]

The process therefore adds up to an attack on the essential meaning of society and the values that hold it together. The artistic influence is cut off once by the elimination of practical craftsmanship and again by the removal of the artist from the day-to-day life of the community. Her or his creativity can neither draw its strength and vision from that collective culture nor feed and inform it in return. The idea of life as organic, as rising up from below rather than being authorised and regulated from above, is entirely inimical to our contemporary capitalist society. Thus it can see no problem with an art driven out of the everyday and shoved into a crystal cage to be jealously guarded and admired by a tiny clique cut off from the wider community. It cannot see that art without roots is dead art.

Coomaraswamy contrasts this modern Western blindness with the Ch'an or Zen art of China and Japan, which recognises its own organic origin by taking for its theme either landscape or plant or animal life. He writes: "Ch'an-Zen art, seeking realization of the divine being in man, proceeds by way of opening his eyes to a like spiritual essence in the world of Nature external to himself; the scripture of Zen is 'written with the characters of heaven, of man, of beasts, of demons, of hundreds of blades of grass and of thousands of trees'... Ch'an-Zen represents all and more than we now mean by the word 'culture': an active principle pervading every aspect of human life, becoming now the chivalry of the warrior, now the grace of the lover, now the habit of the craftsman".[13] Morris likewise states that "everything made by man's hands has a form, which either must be beautiful or ugly; beautiful if it is in accord with Nature, and helps her; ugly if it is discordant with Nature, and thwarts her; it cannot be indifferent".[14]

It is this vital sap of nature, nourished by our cultural soil and flowing into the shoots, leaves and flowers of art, that is blocked by the soulless functionality of industrial capitalist society and its money-minting machineries. Capitalism hates authenticity, hates mystery and thus is utterly incapable of even beginning to appreciate the mystery behind the authenticity of artistic expression or of ever being able to understand why the products of its own system are so sterile and ugly.

The power of this industrial system is so vast that it can, and seemingly intends to, destroy the whole world, and yet it can barely create one tiny item of any genuine value. "Every real work of art, even the humblest, is inimitable," says Morris. "I am most sure that all the heaped-up knowledge of modern science, all the energy of modern commerce, all the depth and spirituality of modern thought, cannot reproduce so much as the handicraft of an ignorant, superstitious Berkshire peasant of the fourteenth century; nay, of a wandering Kurdish shepherd or of a skin-and-bone oppressed Indian ryot".[15] Without this authenticity we are left with what Morris calls the "phantom of *sham* art as the futile slave of the capitalist",[16] or what Coomaraswamy terms "an art which is no longer felt or energized".[17] Walter Benjamin is describing the same loss of inner spiritual essence when he writes that "that which withers in the age of mechanical reproduction is the aura of the work of art".[18]

William Blake, whose own craft as an engraver was threatened by industrialism, understood better than most the magical manner in which a vital, organic, creativity can flow through the individual. Gerald Bullett relates how Blake regarded everyone's life as potentially a continuous work of art:

"Man, as a creature, is a microcosm of the universe of which he is part; and in his creativity he participates in the eternal divine imagining which all creation is. But the creative impulse of man is in chains: the enemies of impulse have persuaded him to neglect or deny his visions, so that his sense of the eternal, of eternity not hereafter but here and now, the reality in and behind all appearances, is dimmed and lost".[19] Read, too, regards the artist as "part of the universal process" and the creative act as resembling the way "the photogenic cells of a plant manufacture certain real substances from the air or the ether or the cosmic rays".[20] Read sees the "spiritual essence in the world of Nature" cited by Coomaraswamy as manifesting itself through the work of the artist who is able to open up and accept its intangible influence. He notes with admiration in the modern artist of his day "the confidence with which he accepts as a gift from the unconscious, forms of whose significance he is not, at the creative moment, precisely aware".[21]

This concept of "forms" is crucial for an understanding of how this admittedly rather vague idea of a spiritual essence might come to be transmuted, via the artist, into something specific and real. Morris describes "forms and intricacies that do not necessarily imitate nature, but in which the hand of the craftsman is guided to work in the way that she does, till the web, the cup, or the knife, look as natural, nay as lovely, as the green field, the river bank, or the mountain flint".[22] These forms may be handed down from generation to generation but they also appear to arise within each individual, drawn up from some well of common sensibility. "Innate Ideas are in Every Man, Born with him; they are truly Himself",[23] writes Blake, in his conviction that we are all born with both a sense of ideal beauty and a moral conscience.[24] Morris ventures that the forms he describes "were once perhaps the mysterious symbols of worships and beliefs now little remembered or wholly forgotten"[25] while Joseph Campbell says that "the shared secret of all the really great creative artists of the West has been that of letting themselves be wakened by – and then reciprocally reawakening – the inexhaustibly suggestive mythological symbols of our richly compound European heritage of intermixed traditions".[26]

Read follows in the neoplatonic footsteps of both Wolfgang Goethe and Carl Jung in regarding the forms inspiring the artist as archetypes rooted in the collective unconscious of humanity. He explains: "Nature, we might say, is a world of plastic forms, evolved or in the process of evolution, and man perceives these forms or carries in his memory images of these forms".[27] The central mystery of art is therefore something much deeper and wider than the individual who physically creates it: "The artist is merely a medium, a channel, for forces that are impersonal".[28] Read depicts the spontaneous emergence of a psychic energy which, passing through the brain, expresses a variety of forms, "the typal forms of reality"[29] by which the universe exists. By giving them a shape and presence on the worldly plane, the artist therefore makes these principles comprehensible to other human beings. He concludes: "Art might therefore be described as a crystallisation of instincts – as the unifying of all feelings and desires; as a marriage of Heaven and Hell, which was Blake's profound intuition of the process. That psychic Energy which is given form by the archetype, Blake defined as Eternal Delight".[30]

A society and mindset which cuts us off from this Eternal Delight, which denies the existence of psychic energy, collective unconscious or archetypal forms, would therefore be inflicting untold damage on the human soul. The "eyeless vulgarity which has destroyed art",[31] to cite Morris, would also be guilty of destroying a fundamental connection between individuals and the spiritual soil in which they are able to grow. And this, indeed, is the debased and despiritualised capitalist society in which we live today, a society in which "everything seems to be increasingly artificial, denatured, and falsified",[32] as René Guénon observes, and in which truth and authenticity are nothing but a distant memory or a seemingly impossible dream.

But just as the condition of art – and its separation from nature, community and the soul – can act as a warning sign as to the state of our world, so it can also perhaps act as a means of righting those wrongs. Read is at pains to explain that his own philosophy of art is to be regarded as part of an attempt to change society for the better and to reclaim all that has been stolen from us by the mechanisms of exploitation. He writes: "If I thought that the world could be saved and the happiness of mankind guaranteed by the sacrifice of aesthetic sensibility, I would not hesitate to accept that sacrifice. But my belief is just the contrary. It is because I see everywhere the threatening shadow of the catastrophe that overtakes a people without vision that I strive to reanimate the only philosophy that can save us".[33]

While condemning the rule of the machine and the "technical coldness" of the early 20th century, Ernst Bloch contrasts its ethos and aesthetics with those of Gothic art, an "elevating spirit" which turns into "organic-spiritual transcendence".[34] That is precisely what we urgently need now if we are to emerge from the darkness of the capitalist age to rediscover the potential richness of our existence – a transcendental spirit rooted in the eternal and organic truth of nature. And there must always be hope. If the spirit of the artist is indeed something that is innate, then it cannot be crushed for ever by external circumstance, only stifled and held down.

It is born again with every new generation, as witnessed by the survival of authentic artistic impulse and sensibility even in the difficult circumstances of current times. When one day the flow of human vitality is once again running unimpeded, we can look forward to the reunification of art with craft and of both of them with the living energies of the universe which it is their role to make visible.

VII

ROMANTIC REVOLUTIONARIES

Such is the potency of the spring waters of the human spirit that even under the factories, railways and endless urban sprawl of the industrial age they always found new fissures through which to find their way to the surface. But to do this, they had to find a way past the very mindset of the period, which could loosely be summarised as positivist.

It is inadequate to treat positivism as a force in its own right, as a self-standing philosophy that just happened to ride in to the rescue of capitalism in the face of a potential spiritual revolt. Positivism is, as we have described elsewhere,[1] *the* philosophy of capitalism, the philosophy that makes it possible. It is indeed no coincidence that the flat "scientific" outlook it promotes is in "perfect harmony with the needs of a purely material civilization".[2]

Positivism lends itself perfectly to an unshakeable faith in the benefits to all of industrialism and "economic growth" – thus providing a very handy "moral" justification for the European conquest and plundering of far-off lands. It makes it easy to see the universe as a machine and the natural world as essentially inanimate. Hills, valleys, rivers and forests whose timeless splendour fed the souls of generations are, from this pragmatic perspective, nothing but potential sources of raw materials. Animals are nothing but moving objects with no feelings, due no respect or care but conveniently placed on the Earth for a superior species to exploit. Even other human beings can essentially be reduced to the role of economic units. Human communities are not organic entities which develop and evolve naturally, like everything else on a living planet, but must necessarily be planned and regulated by Authority, otherwise only uncontrollable chaos could ensue.

The positivist/capitalist mindset is convinced of the rationality, the inevitability, of this course of human collective behaviour. It has defined its Holy Grail of "progress" in such a way that it can only mean the continuation of its own mechanistic system. Its world view is enclosed and self-referential. Any ideas that do not fit in with the tenets of its own faith are denied any validity and, if acknowledged at all, must be dismissed as hopelessly backwards, symptoms of insanity or dangerous threats to the general well-being of an ordered and rational society. These assumptions are built into the intellectual structure of capitalist society and thus into the very way of thinking of the "educated" classes. A positivist outlook becomes synonymous with erudition, intellect, intelligence. Non-positivist ideas are held only by ignorant barbarians and lunatics.

René Guénon remarks that the positivists' "fixed resolve not to tolerate anything that might prove dangerous to accepted opinions, and the attempt to discredit it by every means, alike find their justification moreover in the very prejudices that blind these narrow-minded people, and which lead them to deny the value of anything that is not a product of their own school".[3] Human beings' attempts to find meaning in their own existences are thwarted by the way that philosophy has increasingly been dominated by those who prefer to focus on factual "scientific" detail, laments Guénon: "What interests them is not whether a certain idea is true or false, or in what measure it is so; their only concern is to find out who first propounded the idea, in what terms he formulated it, and at what date and under what accessory circumstances he did so; and this history of philosophy which busies itself exclusively with the scrutiny of texts and biographical details, claims to take the place of philosophy itself, thus bringing about its final divorce from any small intellectually valuable residue that it might have retained in modern times... by clinging to the letter only, it is unable to enter into the spirit".[4]

By the mid-20th century, such restrictions to the scope of permitted thinking had, as Herbert Read notes, resulted in a severe narrowing of the ambitions of human understanding: "The determination of scientists not to ask questions that cannot be answered empirically, and proved logically, has led to a drastic shrinkage of philosophical territory: philosophy is now identified with logic, deductive and inductive, and it is the claim of the scientific philosophers that no other mental activity deserves the name of philosophy. Logical formulas have taken the place of what the scientist calls 'the picture language of speculative systems', and on a diet of such dry dog biscuits modern man is asked to undertake his spiritual Odyssey".[5] Alan Watts complains of exactly the same thing regarding academic philosophers in the UK and USA in the same period: "With their penchant for linguistic analysis, mathematical logic, and scientific empiricism, they have aligned philosophy with the mystique of science, have begun to transform the philosopher's library or mountain retreat into something nearer to a laboratory, and, as William Earle said, would come to work in white coats if they thought they could get away with it".[6]

It was in reaction to the emergence of this positivist thought-monopoly that the 19th and early 20th centuries saw a wave of intellectual resistance swell up. The old stratum of traditional "magical" thinking still lingered, especially in remoter rural areas, and the power of raw rebellion often still arose, only to be crushed. But what emerged was something new, drawing on these rebel traditions and yet finding a contemporary identity of its own. Behind it was an instinctive hatred of the rapidly advancing steam-hammers of industrial capitalism, which were laying waste to the beauties of nature from which people draw their inspiration to live. This was combined with nostalgia for ways of thinking that had been cast aside in the rush for material riches and with an understanding that something must have gone badly wrong in the minds of human beings at some point in the past in order to have led them to the grim present of mills, mines and machinery.

The development of vitalist ideas, reclaiming in a biological context the ancient belief in nature as a living organism, led on to the emergence of an anti-positivist *Lebensphilosophie* expressed by Romantic *Naturphilosophen* such as Carl Gustav Carus (1789-1869), which inspired several generations. This impact was bolstered by the highly influential philosophy of Friedrich Nietzsche (1844-1900), who in 1889's *Twilight of the Idols* condemned "the *despiritualizing* influence of our contemporary scientific pursuits".[7] Richard Noll says of this pivotal period: "A common theme that appears again and again in the documents of that time is the idea that European civilization itself was decaying and dying, that industrialization had stolen the soul of humankind, that disease and death were all that anyone could expect from life".[8] He even suggests that Bram Stoker's novel *Dracula*, published in 1897, was part of this phenomenon: "Dracula, king of the vampires, is the perfect fin-de-siècle cultural horror: something living hundreds of years yet dead, something dead but undead, draining the vitality of the living, like European Civilization itself".[9]

The best-selling status of Ernst Haeckel's 1899 book *Die Welträtsel* (*The Riddle of the Universe*) reflected the rise throughout the 1890s, particularly in the German-speaking world, of "völkisch utopianism based on a rejection of the Christian myth and an emphasis on the worship of nature".[10] "Worship" is not too strong a word, for here was the re-emergence, in a distinctly modern environment, of an age-old belief in the sacredness of the Earth which had somehow survived centuries of repression by the churches and then by capitalism. For the German *Naturphilosophen*, the Earth was "an anthropomorphized entity with its own soul or, indeed, psyche",[11] as Noll remarks: a conviction which, over the course of history, has been the majority one, even if it finds no place in the blinkered outlook of pragmatic industrialism.

The word "worship" also hints at a broader religious and spiritual renaissance which accompanied the rejection of capitalism's empty soullessness. Looking back on the period from 1930, Hanz Kohn recalls: "During the first decade of the 20th century, there was a reawakened interest in Romanticism. Novalis and especially Hölderlin were the most read 'classics' in our youth... For the new generation, specialised and mechanised science seemed cold, lifeless and sterile. We wanted to reach down to the obscure and primordial sources (*Urquellen*) of being... Mysticism was the fountain of youth in which religious nostalgia of the age immersed itself".[12]

Michael Löwy describes this "anti-capitalist Romanticism" as being the dominant force in cultural and academic life in *Mitteleuropa* at that time.[13] He writes: "One of the essential themes of this critique, which resurfaces like an obsession in the work of writers, poets, philosophers and historians, is the clash between *Kultur*, a spiritual realm of ethical, religious or aesthetic values, and *Zivilisation*, the vulgar materialist world of economic and technological progress. If capitalism is, according to Max Weber's mercilessly perceptive expression, the *disenchantment* of the world (*Entzauberung der Welt*), then anti-capitalist Romanticism has to be seen primarily as a despairing and nostalgic attempt at the *re-enchantment* of the world, of which one of the essential dimensions was a return to religion, the renaissance of multiple forms of religious spirituality".[14] Löwy sees this force as manifesting itself everywhere from the writing of Thomas Mann and Theodor Storm or the poetry of Stefan George and Richard Beer-Hoffmann to the *Kathedersozialismus* of Gustav Schmoller, Adolph Wagner and Lujo Brentano, the philosophy of Oswald Spengler and Martin Heidegger or the imagination of the Symbolist and Expressionist movements.

In France, the Symbolist movement reacted against "blinkered rationalism and bourgeois positivism"[15] in a similar way to the German Romantics. Their artistic and cultural revolt also took on a political, or anti-political dimension, with George Woodcock concluding that "in one way or another almost every Symbolist writer was linked with anarchism in its literary aspects".[16] Löwy regards Octave Mirbeau, Laurent Tailhade, Paul Adam, Stuart Merrill, Francis Vielé-Griffin, Camille Auclair and Bernard Lazare as part of a trend towards a revolutionary Romanticism. He writes: "In France, as everywhere else, nostalgia for certain moral values from the past, the idealisation of certain pre-capitalist social forms (rural living or cottage industry) and the rejection of industrial/bourgeois civilization were an essential component of anarchist culture".[17] Lazare, and many of his friends, combined a revolutionary anarchism with an interest in religious, mystic and esoteric ideas.[18]

The same themes appear in Victorian England through the likes of William Blake (1757-1827), William Wordsworth (1770-1850), William Morris (1834-1896) and Richard Jefferies (1848-1887). Jefferies is described by Professor Robin Zaehner (to whom we will return later) as "an outstanding English 'natural' mystic of the nineteenth century",[19] while Gerald Bullet comments that he shows "a sense of communion with an immanent and transcendent reality, to which numberless others through human history – Christians, Moslems, Jews, Hindoos, Taoists, Buddhists, and Agnostics – have also testified".[20] Jefferies' prose particularly encapsulates the mystic sense of a timeless belonging to nature expressed by the Romantics of the period: "From earth and sea and sun, from night, the stars, from day, the trees, the hills, from my own soul – from these I think,"[21] he writes in his best-known work, *The Story of My Heart.*

Morris, disgusted as we have seen by the separation of art and craft in capitalist society, understood the broader context of his own revolt against the spirit of his age, declaring in 1894, two years before he died: "Apart from the desire to produce beautiful things, the leading passion of my life has been and is hatred of modern civilization".[22] As for the other two Williams, Wordsworth and Blake, Bullett explains that they were very different in some ways: "Yet they were at one in essentials; they both strongly repudiated the mechanistic conception of man and nature which prevailed in their day, seeking to replace it in the minds of men by a philosophy that differed from primitive animism (to which it was in some sense a return) in its subtlety of apprehension, its intellectual discipline, and above all its recognition of a unity in all things. For Wordsworth, as for Blake, the universe was alive in all its parts and alive with one life. Nature was *naturans*, not *naturata*: a living organism suffused with that which in its higher manifestations we call mind or consciousness".[23]

One cannot help but feel that what *should* have happened at the dawn of the 20th century was that this great welling up of nausea at the dark deeds of capitalism, born of a primal love of the holistic fullness of life and nature, should have swept away the cast iron foundations of the even-worse nightmare that was to come. The disgust of much of the population of the industrialising world at this toxic departure from health and sanity *should* have been enough to end the experiment there and then and precipitate a new direction for Europe and the world it then dominated, refocusing the intellectual energies of the species on the pursuit of eternal wisdom rather than ephemeral profit. There was a wide range of articulate voices espousing "a kind of pantheistic idealism"[24] – to use a label deployed by Peter Marshall to describe Blake's metaphysics, but which could equally be applied to so many others. Why then did this influential anti-capitalist chorus ultimately fail to reawaken the people and mobilise them to resist the dark destruction being inflicted on them and their world by a small minority of narrow-minded and selfish money-worshipers, crushers of the spirit of humankind and living nature?

Part of the answer tragically lies within the very movement that should have been the vessel for this attack on capitalist industrialism – the radical current that was at the time loosely termed "socialism". Instead of embracing the organic resistance to mechanistic positivism, it turned its back on it. One could perhaps see this as an inevitable consequence of the historical forces at work. If capitalism had spawned a philosophy, in positivism, which answered its own ideological needs then one might expect it also to spawn dissenting traditions that could be contained within its larger framework. The concentration of the means of communication, including publishing, in urban centres could be regarded as part of this self-perpetuating process.

However, some have pointed a finger more specifically at the impact of Karl Marx and his followers on the emergence of a socialist theory which accepted most of the positivist world-view, including the need for economic "progress", had little interest in the land or those who lived on it and certainly rejected any neo-pagan ideas of spiritual attachment to nature. The effects of this ideological positioning went further still, with the abstract conception of human beings in economic terms, and belief in the immediate necessity of a State, negating any holistic notion of a freedom arising from each individual and permeating his or her relationships with other members of a living community.

For 70 years after the Russian Revolution of 1917, Marxism in its varied forms dominated revolutionary thinking across most of the world and its impact on 20th century radical ideology was a heavy and restrictive one. Michael Bakunin had already noticed by 1871 that Marxists "want to see all human history, in the most idealistic manifestations of the collective as well as the individual life of humanity, in all the intellectual, moral, religious, metaphysical, scientific, artistic, political, juridical, and social developments which have been produced in the past and continue to be produced in the present, nothing but the reflections or the necessary after-effects of the development of economic facts".[25] While admirers of Marx will understandably reject criticism of his work based on historical events that occurred long after his death, the authoritarian excesses of the Bolshevik regime in Russia, where Emma Goldman was to witness "the best human values betrayed, the very spirit of revolution daily crucified"[26] at the very least highlight the dangers implicit in this dehumanised, purely economic, view of society.

One forthright opponent of both positivism and Marxism was the German-Jewish anarchist Gustav Landauer (1870-1919). In their insightful analysis of his 1911 text *For Socialism*, Russell Berman and Tim Luke explain that "anticipating certain arguments of the Frankfurt School, Landauer describes modern science's actual function as an identity theory that presumes to describe reality fully, while in fact abstractly manipulating the objective world into total conformity with its formal conceptualizations".[27] They say Landauer saw the need for us to break free from "the false mechanical concepts of science that impoverish human understanding"[28] but understood that Marxism was itself trapped inside this mindset, with its "scientific" belief in the supposedly inevitable transition of capitalism into socialism. This meant orthodox Marxists had to "applaud capitalist growth, for it was precisely that growth, that centralization, and that rationalization of the economy which would sooner or later blossom into socialism, regardless of whether the ballot box or a *coup d'état* ushered in the final phase of human maturation".[29] With its dogmatic faith in the inevitability of Progress, Marxism was in no position to launch a fundamental critique of capitalist industrialization and was itself "part of the problem posed by industrialization".[30] They add: "Marxism, despite its revolutionary appearance, functions in fact as an impediment to socialism... In the light of Landauer's critique, nineteenth century scientific socialism ceases to appear as a radical critique of the *status quo*. Rather, behind its revolutionary pretenses, it buttresses the development of capitalist structures".[31]

In *For Socialism*, Landauer is vehemently outspoken against the Marxists who had taken control of the socialist movement of which he considered himself a part. He describes their dogma as "the plague of our times and the curse of the socialist movement"[32] and declares: "Spirit has been replaced by an eccentric and ludicrous scientific superstition. No wonder that this weird doctrine is a travesty of spirit, since its origin was already a travesty of real spirit, namely Hegelian philosophy. The man who concocted this drug in his laboratory was called Karl Marx. Professor Karl Marx. He brought us scientific superstition instead of spiritual knowledge, politics and party instead of cultural will".[33] He continues: "The Marxists have, in their declarations and views, excluded the spirit for a very natural, indeed almost excellent material reason: namely, because they have no spirit"[34] and bemoans "the grotesque wrongness of their materialist conception of history"[35] in which they reduce everything to "what they call economic and social reality".[36]

Landauer's frustration with the Marxists and the Social Democratic Party in Germany evidently stems from his sense of a lost opportunity, the possibility of a revolution fuelled by the collective spirit, or *Geist*, in the hearts of the people. Thus his dislike of Marxism is not solely based on its "scientific" outlook or its authoritarian potential, but also on its inability to inspire the population, to set in motion the resonance of revolt that was needed to challenge the domination of industrial capitalism. It is a deep disappointment in the betrayal of a broader and deeper movement of resistance that leads him to denounce Marxism as "a negating, destructive and crippling appeal to impotence, lack of will, surrender and indifference".[37]

Ernst Bloch likewise deplores "the positivist spirit in which Marx tore communism out of the theological domain to limit it to the one and only terrain of political economics, thus depriving it of all its millenarianist aspects, both those that have come to it from history and those which are innate to its substance".[38] And Goldman expresses a similar thought when she recalls her first impressions of socialism as "colourless and mechanistic",[39] in stark contrast to the "beautiful ideal"[40] of anarchism to which she was to dedicate her considerable talents and energies for the rest of her life. Bakunin, for his part, identifies a number of "natural traits" ignored by Marxist theory, including "the intensity of the instinct of revolt, and by the same token, of liberty, with which it is endowed or which it has conserved. This instinct is a fact which is completely primordial and animal; one finds it in different degrees in every living being, and the energy, the vital power of each is to be measured by its intensity".[41] How can an ideology that does not understand, or even acknowledge, the primal forces behind the urge for freedom ever hope to inspire people to rise up and claim it for their own?

Landauer also hints at his disquiet over the growing influence of Marxism, and its modes of thinking, on the anarchist movement of the time. He refers disparagingly to "the syndicalists and the anarcho-socialists, recently so-called by a pitiful misuse of two noble names" as the Marxists' "brothers"[42] and specifically extends his condemnation to all Marxists "whether they call themselves Social Democrats or anarchists".[43] This Marxist influence has subsequently often been a matter of contention within anarchist circles, with critics decrying the flattening of a multi-faceted living philosophy into a dry economic dogma. The Russian anarchist Voline and other comrades, for instance, had this to say in response to the

Organisational Platform of the Libertarian Communists, written by the Dielo Truda group of Russian exiles in 1926: "To maintain that anarchism is only a theory of classes is to limit it to a single viewpoint. Anarchism is more complex and pluralistic, like life itself. Its class element is above all its means of fighting for liberation; its humanitarian character is its ethical aspect, the foundation of society; its individualism is the goal of mankind".[44]

As the "Left" became increasingly dominated by Marxist assumptions and focused its hopes on the "inevitable" uprising of the urban proletariat, it had little time for the countryside, whether in terms of the industrial threat to nature or the historically crucial issue of land ownership. As we have seen, it was this initial act of theft against the people that had led to them being reduced to uprooted objects of exploitation in the capitalist machine. But, for an orthodox Marxist, this stage was a necessary one on the long road to socialism. Any thought of a return to the birthright of the land was out of the question and conflicted totally with the Marxist vision of an expanding industrial society in which the means of production were under the (theoretical) collective control of the working class. Landauer was scathing about this gaping hole in Marxist revolutionary theory, insisting: "Socialists cannot avoid the struggle against land ownership. The struggle for socialism is a struggle for the land; the social question is an agrarian question. Now it can be seen what an enormous mistake the Marxists' theory of the proletariat is. If the revolution came today, no stratum of the population would have less idea of what to do than our industrial proletarians".[45]

It was disaster enough that the main ideological force of opposition to capitalism shared many of its assumptions and was thus unwilling, indeed unable, to join forces with the broadly *völkisch* spiritual revolt to bring down what should have been their common enemy. Worse, though, was that, by turning their backs on this *Zeitgeist*, the Marxists and their fellow travellers left it susceptible to be seduced and corrupted by the reactionary forces of the Right, with dire consequences.

VIII

THE WORLD SOUL

There was nothing intrinsically right-wing about the original *völkisch* movement. Its variations included pan-Slavism and early Zionism and even its pan-German branch was largely uncontaminated by the toxic racist creeds that were later to predominate. In fact, its roots are closely entwined with those of the anarchist movement, particularly those of its "alternative" wing.

Richard Noll describes how at the very beginning of the 20th century, "Switzerland and southern Germany became the home of these neopagan, sun-worshiping, nudist, vegetarian, spiritualist, sometimes anarchist, sexually liberated groups experimenting with new life-styles or a new experience-based philosophy of life".[1] Otto Gross (1877-1920), anarchist and renegade psychoanalyst, has been credited for fundamentally influencing Carl Jung (1875-1961) with his theories of sexual liberty and neopaganism[2] and the author Hermann Hesse (1877-1962) "whether he liked it or not – was viewed by many as yet another prominent voice of völkisch mysticism".[3]

The timeless nature religion of the *völkisch* movement had been given a "modern" edge by the anti-Christian Nietzschean philosophy and its injection of a powerful "irrational" critique of conventional society into what was already a heady blend of new ideas. The resulting combination was regarded as extremely frightening by the bourgeois liberal elite, who could see a revolutionary potential that was apparently lost on the Marxists. It was these same ingredients that were to help make up the analytical psychology developed by Jung and his collaborators and set it apart from mainstream, and indeed Freudian, thinking. Noll suggests that one aspect of the divide between Jung and Sigmund Freud was a conflict between their respective "vitalistic Naturphilosophie and mechanistic *Naturwissenschaft* [natural science]".[4]

Emma Goldman, an ardent enthusiast for the works of Friedrich Nietzsche, was clearly influenced, at least in her use of language, by vitalism, the *völkisch* revival and the idea of a collective unconscious. She writes in her autobiography, for instance: "My life was linked with that of the race. Its spiritual heritage was mine, and its values were transmuted into my being. The eternal struggle of man was rooted within me".[5] And in describing the wonderful "tempest of vehement indignation" against the status quo that she encountered on a 1919 lecture tour, she concludes that "it was the eloquent voice of the awakened collective soul, thrilled by new hope and aspiration. We merely articulated its yearnings and dreams".[6]

An even clearer connection can be seen in the philosophy of Gustav Landauer, who, Berman and Luke explain, "sees the folk as living communities of thought and experience which are not explicable in positivist scientific statements"[7] and displays a "characteristic fusion of vitalistic Nietzschean individualism with socialist communalism".[8] It is the fusion of ideas that is of particular interest here, as it points towards a different tradition which could have developed from the early *völkisch* scene, if only the latter had not been estranged from the radical movement by the narrowness of a Marxist ideology whose differences with industrial capitalism were less than fundamental. "Landauer represents a left-wing form of the *völkisch* current in thought," say Berman and Luke. "The turn of *völkisch* thought to the right is ultimately not indicative of the quality of such thought, but rather of the self-imposed constraints of the traditional Marxist left, which failed to appropriate the leftist potential of the *völkisch* movement".[9]

The convergence of *völkisch* and anarchist ideas in Landauer's ideology is at a profound level, encompassing the internationalism that is part of anarchism's deep-seated universalism. Berman and Luke describe the folk consciousness he had in mind as an "inner individual awareness of social ties that demand cooperative activity" which can become a collective mode of existence: "For Landauer, folk consciousness was anything but the chauvinistic élan of nation-state worship that the right-wing *völkisch* movements touted in Wilhelmine Germany".[10] In Landauer's world view, socialism and folk consciousness were essentially the same thing, which is why he was so exasperated by the Marxist abandonment of such an important force for co-operative communal cohesion, which would have had to have been resuscitated in order to allow a free and organic society to re-emerge from the devastation of capitalist industrialism. He writes: "Uprooted, in melancholy strangeness, are the individuals, the few in whom folk-spirit is buried, even if they know nothing of it. Uprooted, divided in hardship and destitution, are the masses into whom the spirit must again flow, if spirit and the people are to be reunited and revitalized".[11]

Among those in whom the folk-spirit resurfaced were a significant number of thinkers who, like Landauer, shared their Germanic cultural heritage with a Jewish one. Noll relates: "Before Pan-Germanism developed into a predominantly anti-Semitic movement at the end of the century, many secular Jews seeking greater political influence through more thorough assimilation into Christian circles (rather than further segregation through Reform Judaism) participated in pan-Germanic activities. The young Freud was such a person, briefly caught up in Pan-Germanism during his student years".[12] However, adds Noll, the anti-Semitism which Freud encountered during this time unsurprisingly ended his interest.

One of those attracted to Ascona, a famed centre of the spiritual counterculture, was Franz Kafka,[13] who met and corresponded with Gross[14] and whose depth of expression Walter Benjamin was later to attribute to "the core of folk tradition, the German as well as the Jewish".[15] Kafka was an active anarchist in his youth, even being arrested and fined in 1912 for taking part in an anarchist demonstration.[16] While his reading reflected this political interest – the Reclus brothers, Domela Niewenhuis, Vera Figner, Michael Bakunin, Jean Grave, Peter Kropotkin and Emma Goldman[17] – other favourite authors belonged to the Romantic anti-bourgeois European tradition, including Arthur Schopenhauer, Nietzsche, Søren Kierkegaard, Gustave Flaubert, Fyodor Dostoevsky and August Strindberg.[18]

The straddling of these apparently separate traditions and their combination with a Jewish background was characteristic, as Michael Löwy has shown, of a very specific philosophical current in Central European thinking that has subsequently been rather overlooked. Löwy describes "a generation of intellectuals born during the last quarter of the 19th century whose writing draws at the same time from German (Romantic) and Jewish (messianic) sources"[19] and who are part of the wider urge to break free from the shallow positivism of the age and find inspiration in "a larger, richer pool of spiritual and cultural thought".[20] He says some of these are religious Jews with anarchist tendencies, such as Franz Rosenzweig, Rudolf Kayser, Martin Buber, Gershom Scholem or Hans Kohn. Others are libertarian revolutionaries with Jewish backgrounds – such as Landauer, Ernst Bloch, Erich Fromm, Ernst Toller and György Luckács. Apart from both, and yet linking them, he places Walter Benjamin. A key part of this loose intellectual movement, or affinity, were the ideals of "an egalitarian community, libertarian socialism, anti-authoritarian revolt, a permanent revolution of the spirit".[21] Löwy adds that the "crushing majority of central European Romantic intellectuals of the utopian-revolutionary variety were Jewish".[22]

It was no coincidence that their German-Jewish philosophy was infused with this particular political flavour. In rejecting pan-German particularism as well as a purely Jewish approach, their sense of organic identity and messianic hopes for "redemption" through revolution both necessarily adopted the universal human perspective that was characteristic of the anarchist outlook. Toller, for instance, declared that if he were to be asked where he belonged, he would answer that "a Jewish mother brought me into the world, Germany fed me, Europe shaped me, my home (*Heimat*) is the Earth, the world is my *Vaterland*".[23] French-Jewish anarchist Bernard Lazare insisted to the prominent Zionist Chaim Weizmann in 1901 that Jewish culture should not mean anything with chauvinistic potential but "on the contrary, must mean culture suited to developing Jewish tendencies which are human tendencies in the highest sense of the word".[24]

Moreover, Löwy points out, there is a definite correspondence between the Jewish religious concept of *Tikkun,* rectification or mending, and the anarchist dream of a revolution combined with restoration: "For Bakunin, Sorel, Proudhon and Landauer the revolutionary utopia always goes hand in hand with a profound nostalgia for forms of the pre-capitalist past, for traditional rural communities or craftsmanship; with Landauer, that even extends to an explicit defence of the Middle Ages... In truth, at the core of the approach of most of the great anarchist thinkers lies a Romantic attitude towards the past".[25]

Many of the writers described by Löwy draw on the mystical tradition not just of the Kabbala and other Jewish sources but of the kind of Christianity that comes closer to the Eastern religions, paganism and neoplatonism. Landauer's vision, in particular, is close to the pantheistic idealism of William Blake and William Wordsworth: in a 1901 essay, *Durch Absonderung zur Gemeinschaft,* he identifies God with *natura naturans,* referring to Meister Eckhart, Spinoza and Goethe.[26]

Löwy notes that there is an element of nostalgia for a lost Golden Age in all revolutionary anti-capitalist thought, but adds that "while with Marx and his disciples this dimension is relativised by their admiration for industry and the economic progress delivered by Capital, with anarchists (who don't at all share this industrialism), it shines out with a particular, unique, intensity".[27] Bloch, a Marxist, was inspired by the realisation that there was an "underground history of revolution" taking in the likes of the Cathars, the Free Spirit movement, Meister Eckhart, the Hussites, Münzer and the Anabaptists, Rousseau and Tolstoy with the aim of doing away with "fear, the state and all inhuman power".[28] But he was distrusted by many of his comrades for this approach and seen as a rather obscure, over-idealistic writer, too immersed in metaphysical speculation and not welded closely enough to a materialist economic analysis of the human predicament.[29]

The same could be said of another very unorthodox Marxist, Benjamin, whom Löwy describes as believing that "revolutionary utopia is reached through the discovery of an ancient, archaic, prehistoric experience".[30] This is not a simple yearning for yesterday, not a proposed return, *retour,* to the past, but a *détour* via the past to a new future. In Benjamin's outlook, says Löwy, "the archaic societies of *Urgeschichte* [the distant past] feature a harmony between man and nature which has been destroyed by 'progress' and is in need of reinstatement in the emancipated society of the future".[31] He adds that, crucially, Benjamin's opposition to Progress isn't issued in the name of conservation or restoration, but in that of revolution.[32]

Löwy has a very clear vision of the existence of anti-capitalist Romanticism as a specific political and cultural phenomenon which "hasn't until now received the attention it deserves because it defies the usual classifications".[33] He says that the demarcation of the political terrain into left/centre/right, conservative/liberal/revolutionary or even regression/status quo/progress effectively excludes the possibility of this particular position.[34]

Also obscured by this restricted view of history are the connections between this universalist Revolutionary Romantic current and the spectrum of ideas that is today often referred to as "Jungian". Landauer very much bridges this apparent gap and draws on the same *Naturphilosophie* when he envisions a socialist society arising from archetypes buried within each individual's psyche, arguing that "all these symbols, in which men bring nature and the self into harmony, are therefore suited to bringing beauty and justice into the communal life of peoples, because they are reflections of the social drive within us, and because they are our own form itself which has become spirit... We have the reality of the living individual communal spirit in us and we must merely let it emerge creatively".[35] One can see a definite continuity here between the thinking of Landauer and that of the English anarchist Herbert Read (1893-1968), himself very directly influenced by Jung, whose works he edited and with whom he struck up an important friendship.[36] Read explains in *The Forms of Things Unknown* that "the archetype predicts a social pattern of behaviour: it is a predilection to forms of action that are latent in the human organism".[37]

These inter-connections offer us a tantalising glimpse of what the *völkisch* and wider Romantic movement could have become, if it had been allowed to feed into the more political forms of revolt against capitalism and its war on both nature and humanity – a set of ideas drawing on the inherited holistic wisdom of the past, invigorated by the freshness of Nietzschean revolt, inspired by the revolutionary thirst for justice and freedom, deepened by an understanding of the symbiotic relationship between individual self-fulfilment and communal harmony. As Benjamin saw, this revolution would not have been the continuation of Progress but its interruption and replacement with a new tradition informed, though never restricted, by the healthy values of the past.

A Romantic movement with a specifically anarchist, or genuine socialist, orientation, and fed by Jewish as well as Germanic cultural springs would have remained defiantly immune from the pollution of right-wing prejudices. Instead, this powerful river of thought was abandoned by those who could have harnessed its force to good and lasting effect and was left to pour its vitality into the stagnant swamps of biological racism and anti-Semitism.

The negative consequences of the Marxist rejection of this current are threefold. Firstly, of course, it meant the socialist movement itself failed to respond to one of the main underlying causes of dissatisfaction with life under capitalism. Secondly, it allowed the Right to exploit that dissatisfaction for its own ends. There was a good deal of deceit involved in the process, for in truth the Right did not really accept much of the *völkisch* outlook but, as ever, its politicians were happy to use popular causes in order to seize power without any intent of seeing them through. Thus the Nazis' apparent love of the countryside translated, once they ran Germany, into the building of motorways right through the middle of it and the further boosting of industrialism with a massive build-up of military capacity. An idealistic love of *Volk* became, in their hands, a murderous hatred of other *Volk*, and the proud *völkisch* ideal of individual and communal freedom and independence was betrayed by the construction of a centralised authoritarian state apparatus that has become synonymous with repression and shared the positivist and Marxist intolerance of any free thought beyond the safe limits of its own dogma. Indeed, Noll recounts that Adolf Hitler "began to persecute the most apolitical of the *völkisch* mystics in order to establish the sole spiritual hegemony of National Socialism as the religion of the

German peoples".[38]

Thirdly, because the *völkisch* element to Nazi ideology was well-known and the complexities of the relationship less so, the entire tradition was retrospectively tarnished by association and, as a result, further distanced from the radical movement of which it could have so easily formed the spiritual wing. In the case of the Jewish strand, the whole culture from which it had arisen was wiped out by Nazism and its members left dead and scattered. The ideal of a Jewish identity intertwined with German roots was yet another victim of the Hitlerian nightmare and Zionism was left as the more obvious political outlet for Jewish Romanticism.

The impact of fascism was similarly damaging to a related school of thought – namely that known as perennialism or traditionalism. Like the *völkisch* movement, this flourished in the vibrant period of intellectual and artistic activity brought to a brutal end by capitalism's Great War, with Mark Sedgwick stating that its origins "lie in the occultist milieu of the Belle Epoque".[39] It, too, rejected the unspiritual foundations of capitalism and the commercial materialism of its age, with its leading figure René Guénon (1886-1951) arguing in *The Crisis of the Modern World* that the principle of quantity had displaced quality in our downward-spiralling contemporary civilization and that, according to traditional Hindu doctrines, "we have in fact entered upon the last phase of the *Kali-Yuga*, the darkest period of this 'dark age'".[40] Elsewhere, he warns of "the illusion of progress among those who, being acquainted with one kind of civilization only, can conceive of no other line of development than their own, believing it to be the only way possible, so that they take no account of the fact that a development in one sense may be largely counterbalanced by retrogression in another".[41] Proposing that the West might seek salvation in the traditional values of its Middle Ages, he joins Benjamin in seeing this as a *détour* rather than a *retour*: "Ultimately it would be a case not purely and simply of copying or reconstructing what existed then, but of drawing inspiration from it in order to bring about an adaptation to suit the actual circumstances".[42]

Although Guénon initially forged links with elements within the Roman Catholic church in France, perennialism was essentially at odds with conventional Christianity, looking instead to an older metaphysics in which the concept of divinity was abstract and immanent rather than anthropomorphic and separate. Unlike the Germanic neopagan movement, however, it was not interested in the specifics of folk culture or attached as a movement to any particular manifestation of esoteric spirituality. Where individuals did immerse themselves in a particular tradition, it was certainly not on account of any supposed biologically inherited cultural affinity. For instance, although Guénon did very much stress the need for an individual to experience esotericism by initiation into, and strict observance of, one spiritual path – a belief that eventually divided him from others, such Frithjof Schuon, who espoused a broader approach – his ultimate choice was Sufism.

There are areas of overlap between the perennialist and Romantic traditions. Ananda Coomaraswamy (1877-1947), one of the most significant perennialists, was an enthusiastic student of the work of William Morris and emulated his guru's *völkisch* leanings by learning Icelandic, a language of epic myths. He was also an admirer of William Blake's idiosyncratic brand of Romantic nature-worship and spirituality. Coomaraswamy was an anarchist, as was the Swedish artist Ivan Aguéli (1869-1917) who introduced Guénon to Sufism.

If perennialism shared, with the *völkisch* and Romantic movement, some connections to anarchism and the radical tradition, it also suffered from subsequent identification with the Right. While the largely apolitical Guénon was specifically anti-nationalist,[43] in keeping with the universalistic nature of his beliefs, some of his ideas were picked up and distorted by Julius Evola, an Italian ultra-conservative who tried and failed to have his neopagan creed of Indo-European warrior initiation accepted into mainstream Fascist and Nazi ideology. This was, of course, very much a departure from the main thrust of perennialist thinking and Evola's fascistic faith bore no relation to the Oriental metaphysics practised by Guénon or indeed to the universal esoteric connections to indigenous North American spirituality explored by Schuon.[44] Mud, however, tends to stick and, combined with a passing interest expressed in Guénon's work by the European New Right,[45] the Evolan offshoot of traditionalism has often served to fend off potential interest in the movement from radical quarters.

Jung has also been criticised for his alleged association, or perhaps lack of disassociation, with the Nazi regime and the apparent ideological connection via the *völkisch* movement of ideas. Noll, however, concludes that there is no real basis to this: "Perhaps what many critics are sensing in Jung is his essential völkisch identity, of which there is much evidence. Jung's is not merely a folk-psychology, but a 'Volk-psychology'. The claimed evidence of the active, open espousal of anti-Semitism or Nazism by Jung is, in my opinion, less directly compelling (hence the greater controversy over it), and is perhaps more fruitfully framed – from the historian's point of view – in its deeper völkisch context. As historians such as Mosse have continually stressed, anti-Semitism and National Socialism, while derivatives of this völkisch tradition, are not to be regarded as completely identical with it and its multiple offshoots, of which Jung and his analytical psychology is only one of many".[46]

In his later work, Jung's mythological emphasis shifted to alchemy and other less specifically Germanic themes, thus diluting grounds for criticism on this account. His belief in a "world soul", humanity's collective unconscious, was inspired by his conversations with black mental patients in the USA, with North American Indians, with Tunisians and with East African tribespeople and was intrinsically universalist.[47]

Moreover, biographer Frank McLynn notes that Jung always had "a deep hatred of colonialism, whether of the formal type practised in the British empire, or the informal 'internal' type practised in the USA, where whites subdued and bullied Native Americans".[48]

That's not to say that Jung has escaped censure on other issues, though. June Singer notes that "on occasion, he has been vilified and discredited by those who needed to deify the gods of rationalism".[49] Indeed Noll, having cleared him of Nazi associations, still apparently considers it a scathing indictment of Jung's movement that it holds "programs and workshops related to New Age spirituality and neopaganism" and that its centres "have been known to offer practical classes or programs on astrology, the I Ching, palmistry, and other practices associated with the occult sciences".[50]

Noll judges that throughout his long career Jung never deviated from the vitalism he had discovered via the *Naturphilosophie* of the Romantics – "even when new discoveries in genetics and other areas seemed to legitimize the predominant scientific worldview of the twentieth century that includes a biology based only on mechanistic materialism".[51] And, striking a somewhat positivist note, he comments that "Jung and his theories have remained well outside the established institutional worlds of science and medicine, as they have been regarded, with justification, as inconsistent with the greater scientific paradigms of the twentieth century".[52]

In this parallel realm of theory and thought beyond the walls of orthodox academia, Jungian ideas blended, in many ways, with the universalism promoted by the perennialist tradition. For instance, Joseph Campbell (1904-1987), an admirer of Jung, and Mircea Eliade (1907-1986), who emerged from the perennialist movement, pursue what are very much complementary approaches in their writings on comparative religion and myth. By the 1960s, memories of the origins of both currents, and the ideological aberrations of their ephemeral right-wing offshoots, had become somewhat obscured by time and they had flowed together into what appeared to be a new stream of alternative holistic thought.

IX

TOTAL REJECTION

Whenever, over the centuries, the stifled collective soul resurfaces and again breathes the invigorating air of contemporary thinking, it does so in a form appropriate to that age. And so it was in the second half of the twentieth century, when lively minds again began to break free from the shackles of the society around them, rejecting the materialist absolutism of industrial capitalism and the consumer society it had imposed on wealthier parts of the world at the expense of the exploited global majority.

Again, there was a renewal of interest in matters of spirit. The writings of Carl Jung were eagerly studied and, as Richard Noll relates, he became "a source of inspiration and affirmation for the neo-pagan religious movements that began to proliferate in Europe and North America during that period – a true Renaissance of the Asconan ideals".[1] Hermann Hesse was transformed, in English translation, from an obscure and already half-forgotten German novelist into one of the voices of the New Age. The holistic mysticism that had fascinated him and his contemporaries was now enthralling a new generation beyond the German-speaking world. A hedonistic attitude was often at the crest of this particular cultural wave and the use of recreational drugs was commonplace in attempts to achieve higher states of mind.

Aldous Huxley was perhaps more of a precursor, than a leading figure, of the 1960s cultural revolution, having published his influential dystopian novel *Brave New World* in 1931, but he was certainly a prominent part of the *Zeitgeist*. In his 1945 work *The Perennial Philosophy* he picks up an intellectual thread left dangling earlier in the century. The title itself makes its sources of inspiration quite clear and Huxley lists no fewer than three books by René Guénon in his bibliography. As well as exploring the roots of this philosophy, particularly in the East, Huxley applies its ethos to the modern world around him and, unsurprisingly, finds that contemporary "wisdom" represents pretty much the opposite of all that is considered of value by the inherited wisdom of humankind.

The cult of technology comes under specific attack: "Technological idolatry is the religion whose doctrines are promulgated, explicitly or by implication, in the advertisement pages of our newspapers and magazines – the source, we may add parenthetically, from which millions of men, women and children in the capitalist countries derive their working philosophy of life... So whole-hearted is the modern faith in technological idols that (despite all the lessons of mechanized warfare) it is impossible to discover in the popular thinking of our time any trace of the ancient and profoundly realistic doctrine of *hubris* and inevitable *nemesis*. There is a very general belief that, where gadgets are concerned, we can get something for nothing – can enjoy all the advantages of an elaborate, top-heavy and constantly advancing technology without having to pay for them by any compensating disadvantages".[2]

For Huxley, as for the tradition he espouses, there is no essential difference between the everyday life of the human being and the cultural or spiritual atmosphere in which he or she lives. Thus he can see the lack of spirituality in the contemporary world not simply in terms of an abstract overview, but on an individual level: "The industrial worker at his fool-proof and grace-proof machine does his job in a man-made universe of punctual automata – a universe that lies entirely beyond the pale of Tao on any level, brutal, human or spiritual".[3] Huxley urges his readers to turn their backs on the empty folly of modern life and reconnect with a tradition that would be our natural birthright, were it not hidden away from us by those who fear its force: "The reign of violence will never come to an end until, first, most human beings accept the same, true, philosophy of life; until, second, this Perennial Philosophy is recognized as the highest factor common to all the world religions".[4]

Huxley continues his philosophical assault on our industrial civilization in a follow-up commentary on *Brave New World* published in 1959. In *Brave New World Revisited,* he highlights the dire consequences of continuing on our current course of endless multiplication and economic "growth", with the spiralling levels of population required to make this possible. He warns that "this fantastically rapid doubling of our numbers will be taking place on a planet whose most desirable and productive areas are already densely populated, whose soils are being eroded by the frantic efforts of bad farmers to raise more food, and whose easily available mineral capital is being squandered with the reckless extravagance of a drunken sailor getting rid of his accumulated pay".[5] He explains that our apparently democratic societies are in fact ruled by a "Power Elite"[6] – "modern technology has led to the concentration of economic and political power".[7]

Huxley also sets out how the apparent physical liberty of the individual in contemporary society can be an illusion. Mental enslavement by a cultural environment introduced to instil obedience and conformity is combined with the warping of the very concept of freedom to the extent that it seems to describe this cerebral servitude. "It is perfectly possible for a man to be out of prison, and yet not free – to be under no physical constraint and yet to be a psychological captive, compelled to think, feel and act as the representatives of the national state, or of some private interest within the nation, wants him to think, feel and act... The victim of mind-manipulation does not know that he is a victim. To him, the walls of his prison are invisible, and he believes himself to be free".[8]

He depicts a possible future in which "democracy" and "freedom" will remain the catchwords of the status quo, but in which at the same time "the ruling oligarchy and its highly trained élite of soldiers, policemen, thought-manufacturers and mind-manipulators will quietly run the show as they see fit".[9] Huxley suggests we should "break up modern society's vast, machine-like collectives into self-governing, voluntarily co-operating groups, capable of functioning outside the bureaucratic systems of Big Business and Big Government".[10]

Opinions of the kind expressed by Huxley were, needless to say, not mainstream and by this stage his viewpoint had already attracted criticism. One noteworthy source of this was a book published in 1957 by Robin Zaehner, Spalding Professor of Eastern Religions and Ethics at the University of Oxford. *Mysticism Sacred and Profane: An Inquiry Into some Varieties of Praeternatural Experience* is, on the whole, informative and scholarly, reflecting its author's academic standing. He is right, for instance, to challenge the use of the term "pantheism" to describe the state of mind, whether held by a nature mystic or a follower of the Hindu Vedānta, of being at one with everything. As he notes, pantheism literally means "all-God-ism" and, since a notion of God does not necessarily feature in the experience, he concludes: "It would be far more accurate to describe the process as 'pan-en-hen-ism', 'all-in-one-ism', for that is what in fact the experience tells us".[11]

While Professor Zaehner particularly criticises Huxley's interest in drug-enhanced mysticism, it soon becomes clear that his objection to Huxley's ideas goes far deeper than this alone and that his differences with other spiritual points of view amount to more than semantics. Indeed, he occasionally lets slip a piece of personal invective that seems out of place in the learned surrounds of his analysis. For instance, he swoops aggressively on a paragraph in *The Doors of Perception* in which Huxley suggests that most people today live such monotonous and limited lives that "the urge to escape, the long to transcend themselves for a few moments"[12] is a natural response. Zaehner condemns this as a "generalization that is typical of the intellectual and particularly of the intellectual who has been born and bred in an industrial civilization".[13] The word "intellectual" is almost invariably deployed in our society as a term of abuse and Zaehner confirms that this is his intent when he argues that Huxley has "greatly exaggerated" the general nature of this urge to escape: "Fundamentally this is only true of the neurotic: it is not true of what William James called the 'healthy-minded', a class to which even now, I am optimistic enough to believe, the great majority of the human race still belongs".[14]

Zaehner goes on to take another swipe at Huxley, declaring that his whole career "predisposed him to conversion to a type of religion that would provide him with a way of escape from a world into which he had found it so extraordinarily difficult to fit himself. He had, it seems, not been a happy man; and because he was both unhappy and introspective, he needed a philosophy or religion that would deliver him from both his unhappiness and himself".[15] Zaehner certainly lays his own ideological cards on the table here by insisting that the very idea that people's lives are so boring as to require some sort of escape is a fallacy, dreamt up by neurotic intellectuals. The "healthy-minded" majority, which presumably includes Professor Zaehner of Oxford University, have no problem at all living in the same industrial civilization, he claims, and thus have no need to escape in any way. The philosophies adopted by Huxley and his like are therefore nothing but mental devices used to fend off the realisation of their own personal inadequacies.

The assault does not end there. Zaehner claims that he has been "forced to the conclusion" regarding nature mysticism that "if not identical with the 'manic' state in the manic-depressive psychosis, then at least it is its second cousin"[16] and even that "there is a definite connexion between nature mysticism and lunacy".[17] Warming to his theme, he judges that one passage from the Hindu Upanishads "seems to be based on a praeternatural experience akin to acute mania"[18] and that some Sufi thinkers from the esoteric Islamic tradition are "purely paranoiac cases".[19]

Manic, paranoiac, lunacy? Zaehner's insulting tone takes on a patronising hue when he assesses the merits, or otherwise, of spiritual traditions beyond his own Christianity. He writes, for instance, of the ancient texts of Hinduism: "The mere fact that the Upanishads are revered as a sacred book by hundreds of millions should not blind us to the fact they are the efforts of relatively primitive men to discover an adequate philosophy of the universe".[20] The terms "efforts" and "relatively primitive" point to a certain cultural arrogance on Zaehner's part. His conclusion that the early Hindu development of the abstract concept of Brahman "shows that a genuine apprehension of one eternal and changeless Being was already in progress"[21] strikes the same chord, assuming as it does that the Christian concept of God is the highest rung on some kind of evolutionary metaphysical ladder.

Essentially, his issue with nature mysticism, Hinduism and other forms of what he terms "monism" is that they are not the same as Christianity. This stance leads in some peculiar directions, such as when he argues that the elation felt by a nature mystic is a potentially dangerous state of mind, adding: "Christian mystics may well be referring to this experience when they speak of the Devil's ability to counterfeit mystical states".[22] Likewise, he approvingly quotes Jan van Ruysbroeck, the medieval cleric who complained that the Brethren of the Free Spirit "know no internal submission to anything" (*see*

Chapter 3), in his view that "false" mystics are "all the forerunners of Antichrist".[23] So, for all his academic qualifications, Zaehner is falling back here on the argument that anyone embracing forms of mystic experience beyond the Christian one is either insane or in league with the Devil. This was the same line used by Martin Luther's henchman Philipp Melanchton to condemn Thomas Münzer and is an approach that would have been all-too familiar to those accused of witchcraft or other forms of heresy by the Church and its inquisitors in previous centuries.

Given his strong antipathy to ideas challenging Christian orthodoxy, it is hardly surprising that Zaehner also takes offence at the ideas promoted by Carl Jung. He is not alone in this. As we have seen, Jung's view of the world can be traced back partly to late 19th century neopaganism. Noll, in his critical study of Jung, tries to somewhat have his cake and eat it when, in addition to criticising Jung's allegedly irrational and unscientific approach, he also attempts to portray in a negative light the Jungian divergence from the Judeo-Christian religious tradition, not itself known for its scientific rationalism, as we noted earlier. Portraying the concept of an inner divinity as a form of "self-deification",[24] Noll comments in scandalised tones: "Jung's psychological theory and method, which are so widely promoted in our culture today, rests on this very early neopagan or völkisch formulation – a fact entirely unknown to the countless thousands of devout Christian or Jewish Jungians today who would, in all likelihood, find this fact repugnant if they fully understood the meaning behind the argument I make here".[25] He refers to "Jung's vigorous rejection of the Christian god and his guerilla war against the organized Judeo-Christian religions of his day".[26]

Zaehner, too, is evidently aware of the anti-Christian implications in Jung's work, though his criticism is initially a little oblique. Having discussed the poet Arthur Rimbaud's concept of an "other" or a "greater than he" directing his life, Zaehner concludes that this is "in fact nothing other than the 'collective unconscious' of Jung which, in its turn, seems to be identical with the Mind at Large of Huxley".[27] Zaehner then claims that the Jungian collective unconscious is equivalent to the Sufi idea of the *nafs* or lower self[28] and thus not worthy of elevation to a higher level of reality. He argues that "modern psychology is the science of the sick psyche, not of the immortal spirit which the nature mystic experiences beneath it. It is the science of the 'lower soul' of the Muslims, and does not, and presumably cannot, touch the 'higher soul' or spirit which all religions affirm to be immortal".[29] However, here he is confusing separate concepts. The "sick psyche" of the patient is not the *same* as the collective unconscious, although its *relation* to the collective unconscious may be examined. Furthermore, Jung very deliberately uses the word "unconscious" rather than "subconscious" to make it clear that the term does not simply refer, as Zaehner assumes, to the "lower self" but to the whole spectrum of supra-individual concepts, archetypes and so on, which are available to nourish the personal mind. This could as well be regarded as a "higher" self as a "lower" one, although the concept is best not expressed in such terms at all.

Zaehner is right to say that "Jung's integrated personality... is still only on the individual level",[30] rather than on the collective one, but then the specific aim of the psychological process is contained within that particular reality. This does not preclude – and indeed in a Jungian context, positively must include – the existence of a collective unconscious to which the individual is related in various ways. Indeed, Zaehner's own use of the word "level" indicates that the effort to achieve an "integrated personality" cannot be seen as self-contained. The everyday Jungian psychology, used to treat patients, is just the pragmatic manifestation of a deeper philosophy that operates on many levels. The professor of religion could hardly have been unaware of the ancient idea of microcosm and macrocosm, even if it does not feature prominently in his own Christian faith.

Zaehner's concern that the question of "the problem of evil"[31] is not adequately addressed either in Jung's philosophy or in Hinduism[32] also appears to be a misunderstanding of the nature of these beliefs. For a Christian, "evil" is an absolute reality, whereas from other perspectives the term may only be seen as applying to specific actions, or modes of behaviour, and ceases to register as a separate entity once one has risen from consideration of human life to contemplation of abstract notions of being.

Similarly, Zaehner seems lacking in insight when he repeatedly argues that the experience of a nature mystic is incompatible with the mystic experience of feeling at one with the cosmos. He insists that "the exclusion of all that we normally call Nature" is the *sine qua non* of a higher form of mystical experience[33] and at one point asks: "How can a sensation, the essence of which is to feel that one actually *is* the outside world, be identical with the result of a technique which uncompromisingly separates the immortal soul from all sensible images?"[34] Again, this apparent contradiction presents no problem for those not viewing it from a hostile philosophical position. It all comes back to levels again. On one level we can feel at one with humanity, with nature, with all that surrounds us in the visible world and on another level, and another occasion, we can feel that all this is illusory in comparison with the greater cosmic unity that we may occasionally be lucky enough to momentarily grasp.

For Christians there is a gulf between God and his Creation. Divinity and Nature are not identical. But for those who believe that nature is itself "divine", there is no contradiction in embracing nature *en route* to embracing divinity. As René Guénon explains, in Vedāntan metaphysics the multiplicity of worldly existence "is based upon unity, from which it is derived and within which it is principially contained".[35] This position is not the direct pantheism of seeing "God" in everything around us and yet it still accounts for what Zaehner wrongly regards as a contradiction. "It is solely in principle that all things are *Brahma*", stresses Guénon, "but also it is that alone which constitutes their fundamental reality".[36] Attempts to understand such concepts by those who are used to a rather limited way of thinking (such as that promoted by Christianity, as well as by positivism) tend to resemble, to paraphrase Fritjof Capra, efforts to apply two-dimensional geometry to the surface of a spherical planet.[37] It just doesn't work, but if you continue to believe that the world is flat, you are never going to understand why.

Again, Zaehner appears not to properly grasp Jung's concept of people having two "poles" (yin/yang, female/male and so on) to their personality, commenting that "between the two poles, according to Jung, lies sanity and integration".[38] Not really. The idea of polarities is that they are transcended and embraced, not that some mid-point between them is arrived at. But then that realisation requires more than one-dimensional thought.

In the latter part of *Mysticism Sacred and Profane,* Professor Zaehner reveals the core of his argument and the essential reason why he has such a problem with the Perennial Philosophy espoused by Huxley, as well as with Jungian neopaganism and spiritual traditions such as Hinduism. He complains, regarding the Vedānta, that "a system develops which, by insisting overmuch on the absolute unity of being and the absolute reality of the human soul, is forced to identify the two completely, thereby excluding God as an ontological impossibility".[39] One can appreciate that this exclusion would itself be of concern for a believer, but there is a deeper level yet to Zaehner's hostility to non-Christian spirituality. He remarks, with alarm, again of the Hindu tradition: "On the premises of the Māndūkya Upanishad there can be no humility or sense of awe in the face of an Absolute Being who alone really exists and is distinct from man: there can be no sense of nullity or of unworthiness".[40] Here, it seems, we have the crux of the matter: Zaehner believes that humans should feel a "sense of nullity or of unworthiness" when confronted with divine Authority, which should be kept separate and distant for this purpose.

At this point, it may be enlightening to take a brief look at Professor Zaehner's own life, in search of some understanding of this rather startling ideal for the human psychological state. Before he took up his tenure at Oxford, he was a diplomat working for MI6, the British intelligence service, both during and after the Second World War. In 1949 he helped train anti-Communist Albanians as part of a failed attempt to recover British and American control of that Balkan state. He also worked alongside the CIA to plan the coup which brought down the elected government of Iran in 1953, restoring the Shah and returning nationalised oil production to the Anglo-Iranian Oil Company, later to be known as BP. Journalist Robert Fisk writes that "the plot to overthrow Mossadeq and give the oil fields back to the AIOC was in the hands of a British diplomat called Robin Zaehner, later a professor of Eastern religions at Oxford".[41] Back in Britain after his adventures, Zaehner marked the start of his Oxford career by delivering an inaugural lecture strongly criticising the concept of universalism in religion.

We have here the context which goes some way to explaining Zaehner's abrasive approach to the ideas of Huxley, Jung and non-Christian religions. He was very much an Establishment man and, with his post-war activities, had firmly nailed his colours to the mast of British neo-colonialism. We have already seen in Chapter 5 that the British Empire regarded Hindu beliefs as such a threat to the submissiveness of its subject people that it was prepared to promote a compliant Indian "protestantism" to take its place. From that perspective, the growing interest in alternative forms of spirituality presented a similar threat, or perhaps the same threat, but this time much closer to home. Where would we be without a sense of "unworthiness" to keep populations in their place? How could the Empire be held together if the very idea of Authority was being challenged on a fundamental metaphysical level?

Armed with this insight into Zaehner, the man, we can see a very political bias behind his criticism of Huxley, when he writes: "Huxley's life would appear to have been one consistent revolt against the values of the nineteenth century, purely material values to which an air of respectability was lent by a decadent Christianity... We can only conclude that Huxley's 'conversion' to a Vedāntin way of life was due to little more than a total rejection of everything that modern civilization stands for and to a deep-seated aversion to historical Christianity which, though it may not have directly given birth to the modern world, at least condoned it when it was born".[42] Lack of awe in the face of Authority and a total rejection of everything that modern civilization stands for – these are cultural trends to send a shiver down the spine of any authoritarian neo-imperialist, such as Zaehner.

It would seem that he had the intelligence to see where ideas like Huxley's and Jung's could lead and was, when he published *Mysticism Sacred and Profane* in 1957, already declaring ideological war on the cultural revolution of the 1960s, in which the pillars of conservative capitalist society in the West seemed to come tantalisingly close to collapsing. The power of that amorphous uprising stemmed from the fact that it was not confined to a purely political level, but represented a deeper sea-change in social attitudes. At the core of it was the ideal of freedom. As Huxley wrote at the end of the previous decade, when the first tremors of revolt were already being felt: "Some of us still believe that, without freedom, human beings cannot become fully human and that freedom is therefore supremely valuable".[43]

Some of us, yes. But unfortunately there will always also be those who, for some reason, do not feel the same way. For them, there is no life-affirming inspiration in the call to liberty, no joy in the realisation of the essential oneness of the cosmos, no sense of eternal empowerment in the understanding that we individuals are beautiful but ephemeral blossoms on the timeless tree of life. For them, all such talk is dangerous, insane, devilish and should not be allowed to turn the heads of the "healthy-minded" and humbly obedient majority. Who knows what personal circumstances must have combined to produce such a negative, passive, life-resistant mentality, but one can surely feel pity as well as repulsion at the mindset of someone like Professor Robin Zaehner who can muse, without any apparent sense of unease, that "there comes a point in most lives when one tires of the ceaseless responsibility of having to act and choose, and one longs for a higher power to take over the direction of one's life even if the higher power is only the army or a party organization".[44]

X

A CRIME AGAINST HUMANITY

We began this book by considering the idea of Authority and how it somehow became an accepted part of human existence. For those who believe in the fundamental freedom of each individual, and thus of the collective as well, it is hard to understand why that fine concept does not instead lie at the heart of our society. However, we have arrived at an important juncture with the encounter, in the last chapter, of a point of view that specifically wishes humanity to be dominated by a "sense of nullity or of unworthiness".

Looking back over the preceding chapters, this animosity to liberty perhaps lies at the root of all the wrongs that have been inflicted on humanity for so long. It isn't just the land from which we have been cut off, or its supply of free food, or even the culture and cohesion that comes with it, but the whole universe. The traditional holistic view regards humanity as part of an all-embracing whole. This may contain a more abstract transcendent level that could be termed divinity, but this one-ness very much – quite necessarily, in fact, if it is a one-ness – contains within it the material world.

For a religion such as Christianity, divinity is set apart from the universe it has created. This means that divinity is also set apart from humanity. We can have a relationship with this divinity, but it will be one based on reverence, worship, fear – a sense of unworthiness in fact. It is made quite clear in this kind of non-holistic religion that we are certainly *not* part of the divinity in any way and should never dare to consider ourselves such. Neither should we ever regard nature and the world around us as divine. We are not supposed to find any divinity in ourselves, our fellow human beings, certainly not in other living creatures, or in our surroundings. Our only spiritual connection is supposed to be through the authorised channels of the religion in question, through its rituals and representatives.

This is disempowerment to a simply overwhelming degree and we can see echoes of it throughout all areas of life in this flattened-out, lifeless desert of a human culture we term our civilization. Authority is something that must be seen as emanating from above. Even when authority is supposedly invested in the public, in a "democratic" society, it can never be left to emerge from below in a natural sort of way. Instead there must be structures which theoretically transmit the opinions of individuals through complex filtering systems of representation until they pop up at a level of power above that of the individual or even the community, in the form of a new kind of authority, a "democratically-elected" authority. One cannot argue with this kind of authority, any more than one could argue with the old kind. In fact, it is an even worse sin to deny *its* divinity, as by doing so one also denies "democracy" and the supposed rights of citizens to shape the world in which they live.

Faced with, for instance, the risk of some horrific industrial process poisoning their water supply, citizens of a "democratic" state are not supposed to simply get together and stand in front of the building site to stop it going ahead. If they do, they will be punished by Authority for not following the rules set down by Authority. They should have gone through the proper channels. They should have somehow voted somebody into Authority who wasn't going to allow this thing to take place, or they should have formed their own Authority-respecting political party and stood for election in a bid to become Authority themselves and stop the thing from happening. If they haven't done that, then all they can do now is to write to those who do represent Authority and beg them, in a respectful and humble tone, reflecting their own innate unworthiness, to change their minds.

If they go ahead and defy Authority, then Authority has, of course, the right to lock them up. This is a right that Authority has awarded to itself. And since a critical mass of people seem to accept that it has that right, it can essentially behave as it wishes. People are also taught to be afraid of what would happen if there were no Authority any more, nobody to make and impose the rules, nobody to look up to and fear. The idea of people reaching decisions themselves on a communal level, without any interference, is regarded as absurd.

If one believes, as the holistic tradition does, that all life is divine, that we are of a "common essence", that authority resides in ourselves and not on some separate invented level of reality, then a free society sounds like a good idea. But not, however, if one is promoting the idea that without Authority from above there would be chaos and that all life is not divine at all, but is just base matter dependent for its meaning and form on a separate and superior authority figure. Bestowing an overriding sense of value on this base matter would amount to nothing less than turning the world upside-down and would have to be condemned in the strongest terms possible within the dominant thought-system. As Joseph Campbell confirms: "The biblical representation of God as somebody 'up there', not the substance, but the maker of this universe, from which he is distinct, had deprived matter of a divine dimension and reduced it to mere dust. Hence, whatever the pagan world had regarded as evidence of a divine presence in nature, the Church interpreted as of the Devil".[1]

Where there is an "above" occupied by God and Authority,

there is also a "below" that the rest of us we are told we belong to, like it or not. The protestant John Calvin's mind was, according to Gerald Bullett, "dominated by two ideas: the transcendent sovereignty of God and the utter depravity of Man"[2] and he was not alone in that infliction. The overall dualistic Christian message is thus that nature is not in the least divine, has "no virtue in it whatsoever"[3] and that "life in its spontaneity is not innocent but corrupt".[4] Compare this with Carl Jung's belief that "the substance that harbours the divine secret is everywhere, including the human body. It can be had for the asking and can be found anywhere, even in the most loathsome filth".[5] In the ninth century, Johannes Scotus Erigena was expressing similar thoughts. Says Bullett: "Erigena's *natura* stands, not for Nature in our limited sense, but for the totality of all things, both created and uncreated. The material universe is nothing more or less than the necessary self-manifestation of God".[6]

The same life-affirming vision has been expressed over and over again throughout human history, whether by shamans, Greek philosophers, Hindus, Buddhists, Taoists, neoplatonists, medieval magicians, Brethren of the Free Spirit, Ranters, alchemists, *Naturphilosophen*, perennialists or contemporary neopagans. As the divisive Christian dogma disempowers, so the holistic vision empowers – and it frightens those who nurse a "dread of pantheism",[7] every time that it resurfaces. Jan van Ruysbroeck, the authority-loving Christian, encountered the mystic Beghards in the Middle Ages and complained: "They maintain that they are free, and united with God without mean, and that they are advanced beyond all the exercises of Holy Church, and beyond the commandments of God, and beyond the law".[8] Benjamin Whichcote entered Emmanuel College, Cambridge, in 1626 and was immediately criticised by his tutor for "his emphasis on the inwardness of authority",[9] sparking off a long war by the university establishment against the dangerous ideas of this Cambridge platonist.

Repeatedly, it becomes clear that freedom is incompatible with the ways of the Church, even when expressed within an ostensibly Christian context. The very idea of morality in Christianity is dependent on definitions of Good and Evil, laid out by the authority of the Church. The concept of an innate code of behaviour emerging in an authentic human collectivity is as alien to the orthodoxies of Christianity as to those of Marxism.

It is, however, an essential part of other world views, such as of Taoism. Alan Watts writes about the concept of *wei* as "forcing, meddling and artifice" – which seems to amount to much the same thing as Authority. *Wu-wei*, on the other hand, is "not forcing" or "going with the grain". He concludes: "*Wu-wei* is thus the life-style of one who follows the Tao, and must be understood primarily as a form of intelligence – that is, of knowing the principles, structures, and trends of human and natural affairs so well that one uses the least amount of energy in dealing with them. But this intelligence is, as we have seen, not simply intellectual; it is also the 'unconscious' intelligence of the whole organism and, in particular, the innate wisdom of the nervous system".[10]

So how have we reached this state of affairs in which the human organism has lost natural control of itself and is now in the hands of an abusive minority? Part of the success of Authority has been to disguise its own role and to make it appear that the unhealthy situation we have for so long experienced is in fact healthy and natural. For as long as people see their opinions as being derived from some external source, they are capable of suddenly distancing themselves from those views and rediscovering their own personal response. But if, however, they have come to accept a certain view of the world as being "just the way it is", and have no awareness that there is any subjectivity involved at all, it requires a vast mental leap to break free from that illusion. Unquestioning acceptance of the official Christian faith, although enforced by centuries of repression as we have seen, became the norm in Europe and reached a level of stability where it became self-perpetuating within society. The Christian view of the world was taken for granted, as the Muslim view might still be in many countries.

Although Christianity is not totally accepted in Europe today, the way in which it retained its control has been replicated by the dominant contemporary thought-system of capitalist materialism. This system is, as we have seen, equally hostile to the idea of a living planet and universe, insisting that human thought should obey the laws which it has authorised and rejecting anything that strays beyond that and thus might challenge its monopoly on our conception of reality. The majority of people who abide by this metaphysical *diktat* are not consciously bowing to the authority of mechanistic positivism, but have simply absorbed and uncritically accepted its assumptions in the same way as their ancestors went along with Christianity.

Such is the penetration of this mindset into their own thinking, that ideas beyond its narrow confines not only appear wrong, but laughably, absurdly, even unthinkably wrong. "Most of those millions of persons who today would laugh at the idea of magic or miracles would have difficulty in explaining why. They are victims of society's constant pressure towards intellectual conformity,"[11] writes Keith Thomas. The same principle applies on the political level. Rebecca Fisher explains how the dominant system perpetuates the idea "that democracy and capitalism are not only compatible, but indivisible" and thus instils "the widely held belief that challenging capitalism is not only misguided but unprogressive, even pernicious, and as a result, deserving of the marginalisation and repression it receives. This ideological perversion of 'democracy' is therefore used to create a hegemonic order in which a set of beliefs which broadly correspond to the 'democratic' nature or at least potential of capitalism becomes so accepted, even internalised, throughout the public mind that it acquires the status of 'common-sense' or even of a self-evident 'truth' and thus opposing values or ideas are deemed 'illegitimate' or 'unacceptable' or even 'illogical'".[12]

Given the penetration of this mind-control into the collective social psyche, so sophisticated that it hides its own tracks and is not even recognized as existing by its victims, how could we ever begin to challenge it? Campbell, for one, does not seem certain that we can. He regards us, today, as living in a Waste Land where "the myth is patterned by authority, not emergent from life"[13] and where "force and not love, indoctrination, not education, authority, not experience, prevail in the ordering of lives".[14] He warns: "Coerced to the social pattern, the individual can only harden to some figure of living death; and if any considerable number of the members of a civilization are in this predicament, a point of no return will have been passed".[15]

One could retort, however, that the idea of a "point of no return" makes no sense within a holistic tradition in which the cyclical nature of life is constantly emphasised. The prevailing system of Authority, in all its many guises, has needed to make an enormous effort, over many centuries, to keep down the vital spirit of humanity and we have no reason to think that this surge of liberating will is not born anew with each new generation, regardless of external circumstances. Mircea Eliade argues that "the roots of freedom are to be sought in the depths of the psyche, and not in conditions brought about by certain historical moments" and therefore that "the desire for absolute freedom ranks among the essential longings of man, irrespective of the stage his culture has reached and of its forms of social organisation".[16]

Our collective task is thus simply to allow the love of freedom to blossom in our hearts and mind. The first step in this process must be to undo the profoundly damaging effects of the mental separation of divinity and nature by reaching not just an understanding but a knowledge, a *gnosis*, that we and everything around us are all part of one Whole. We are all contained, at the higher levels of metaphysical abstraction, within an all-embracing unity that might be equated with divinity but really belongs to a conceptual stage far removed from that notion as traditionally grasped in the West. We have to feel, deep within ourselves, what Pierre-Joseph Proudhon describes as "a secret connexion between our soul – and through it the whole of Nature – and the infinite".[17] This realisation may or may not come within the framework of an existing religion or philosophy, although in most cases a significant rupture from sterile orthodoxy will be required.

It could also come from the wonderful sensation, which often transports the human mind into delightful rapture, of deep attachment to the natural world. "It was as if everything that had seemed to be external and around me were suddenly within me," writes the Irish novelist Forrest Reid of this mystic experience. "The whole world seemed to be within me... A cloud rose in the sky, and passed in a light shower that pattered on the leaves, and I felt its freshness dropping into my soul, and I felt in all my being the delicious fragrance of the earth and the grass and the plants and the rich brown soil. I could have sobbed with joy".[18] Watts likewise attests that when he is surrounded by nature "I feel this whole world to be moved from the inside, and from an inside so deep that it is my inside as well, more truly I than my surface consciousness".[19] Ultimately, whatever route we take, we will have shared the all-illuminating insight of the Sufi mystic Bayazid, when he declares: "Then I looked and I saw that lover, beloved, and love are one!"[20]

The result of this insight goes far beyond a theoretical comprehension of the reality of the world and our place in it and amounts to an emotional re-discovery of oneself and one's potential, as if the sluice-gates of individuality had been opened and the great expansive force of the universe allowed to flood joyfully through one's veins. There is, as Bullett set out, "a loss of separateness, a sense of union with all spirit, and an intuition or sensation of immortality, not necessarily of one's own immortality as a local and individual person, but rather of an immortal reality to which one already belongs".[21]

How could we begin to estimate the impact such a revelation would have, if experienced not just by a handful of mystics, but by huge swathes of the population freed at last from the chains of restrictive thinking? Important change does not always happen in dribs and drabs. Sometimes, particularly when its inevitability has been dammed up and artificially delayed, such as by the desperate efforts of Authority to maintain its control, it takes the form of a great tidal wave, sweeping away every obstacle in its path.

We do not live in a society mainly populated by happy and fulfilled people. Most of us secretly yearn for an opening-up of life, for our experience of it to become vivid, full-blooded and intoxicating, rather than pallid, tame and relentlessly boring in the way daily existence under the industrialist yoke tends to be. In a world where so many people are looking for "something" – and failing to find it in all the various inadequate substitutes offered to us by society – we have every reason to expect them to be attracted to a psychological path that Richard Noll describes as "Jung's promise of liberation, of freedom, of becoming a continually self-re-creating individual in a state of constant becoming, a perpetual revolution of the soul".[22] On that path our vision will no longer be blocked by the walls of hateful negativity that tell us we are depraved and corrupt sinners, born to be nothing but humble and obedient slaves. It will allow us to break through the illusion of a separate divinity contrasted with an unworthy humanity and know that we ourselves form part of the undivided glory of the living cosmos. When we have done so, we will also find, lying shattered into tiny shards, the insidious lie that Authority is anything other than a crime against life itself.

XI

THE SPIRAL OF HOPE

Deep anxiety is a common personal reaction to the world stripped of meaning and authenticity in which we find ourselves today. One solution proposed for this crisis of the spirit is to "live in the Now" and thus put into some kind of distant perspective the nagging confusions of our contemporary society, to root oneself in the physical reality of each moment, finding a firm foundation in the sensations of looking, listening, breathing, walking, eating.

Living in the Now is to experience reality very much on the axis of time: in fact to surf along it on the wave of the present. There are, however, other axes we could use as the foundation for a living that is not left floating in meaningless mid-air. One of these is the axis of place. As descendents of people thrown off the land many generations ago, we may lack the connections that would have been enjoyed by our more distant ancestors, but we still derive meaning from geographical location. There are the places where we grew up, to which we perhaps still often return in our dreams and which therefore, in some ways, we never leave. There are the significant places in our lives, which we revisit after 10, 20 or 30 years and find haunted by the friends, lovers and events of our past. Places also often have a spirit of their own, an identity which we can tap into when we're there and which can linger on in our minds long after.

We can locate another axis in people. When we think of someone we know well, we don't just think of them as they are today – our mental picture is informed by layer upon layer of experience, memory and judgement. It is not easy for us to change an opinion of somebody that has been built up over time, for better or for worse. Even if they have in fact fundamentally evolved since we formed that view, we may never fully abandon our basic conception of who they are and replace it with the updated version.

These axes on which we can build our understanding of the world – and the above are some basic examples – act as links between separate experiences and themes. We can see various times and places in our lives as being linked by the fact that we were there with a particular person. We can see various times and people in our lives as being linked through a particular place. All these axes and intersections form a living network of meaning from which we can make sense of our lives.

Even on a theoretical level, then, we can see that it would be foolish to attempt to live along one such axis to the detriment of all the others. A blinkered obsession with a particular place, or with a particular person, can blind us to the myriad of meanings and possibilities in life and severely limit our potential. The same is true with time. An obsessive nostalgia for the past is unhealthy for any individual, of course, but so is the addiction to the present moment that results from living excessively in the Now. It encourages a drifting and passive kind of experience, dependent on unthinking reaction to immediate stimuli. Despite the intention of shedding the ambitious and anxious ego, the Now personality can become selfish by paying no attention to others' needs, to the importance of commitments, relationships and plans, simply glorying in the irresponsible spontaneity of its own eternally present tense. It may manage to avoid anxiety in this way, but only by ignoring the fact that anxiety is a symptom. The root causes of the problem are simply ignored and any real remedial action indefinitely postponed.

What applies to the individual also applies to the macrocosm of society. Collectively we are also tempted to retreat into living purely in the Now, in the face of the disorientating storm of anxieties swirling around us. Living perpetually in the present tense of the News, we simply respond intuitively to the stimuli it offers, find ourselves carried along from one issue to the next. Attempts to reach a deeper long-term understanding of our collective predicament are made virtually impossible by the constant white noise generated by accounts of history serving the interests of the status quo. Sometimes it's merely the sheer amount of irrelevant detail that makes it difficult to make out any real shape to what's been happening to humankind, but often these accounts are deliberately misleading.

Los Amigos de Ludd write that capitalism imposes its own reality by "reducing History to a succession of stages in the fulfilment of its own dogma, and the past to a skeleton of concepts and abstractions".[1] For Herbert Read, our understanding has been defeated by "the abdication of philosophy, its retreat into verbal analysis; the inadequacy of scientific rationalism; and finally the dehumanization of art".[2] And Michael Löwy sees all this as emanating from a ubiquitous contemporary philosophy which has coloured all points of view from conservatism to liberalism, social-democracy to communism, authoritarianism to democracy, reaction to revolution, colonialism to anti-colonialism: "Based on a strictly quantitative conception of temporality, it sees the movement of history as a continuum of constant improvements, of irreversible evolution, of growing accumulation, of beneficial modernisation for which scientific and technological progress provides the motor".[3]

In contrast to this official story of Progress are visions such as Walter Benjamin's famous imagining of the angel of history, as inspired by Paul Klee's painting *Angelus Novus*. "His face is turned towards the past," explains Benjamin. "Where we perceive a chain of events, he sees one single catastrophe which keeps piling wreckage upon wreckage and hurls it in front of his feet. The angel would like to stay, awaken the dead, and make whole what has been smashed. But a storm is blowing from Paradise; it has got caught in his wings with such violence that the angel can no longer close them. This storm irresistibly propels him into the future to which his back is turned, while the pile of debris before him grows skyward. This storm is what we call progress".[4]

Like Benjamin, we need to be able to step back from the frantic ever-changing detail of the Now and see that it is part of a much broader and more significant scenario. The attempt in these pages has been to provide a particular axis from which we can view the past and present of humankind, to reveal a seam in the rock of history which might tell us something about where we are. It has revealed a humanity dispossessed, a society in which freedom, autonomy, creativity, culture, and the spirit of collective solidarity have been deliberately suffocated by a ruthlessly violent and exploitative elite hiding behind the masks of Authority, Property, Law, Progress and God.

Such enslavement of humankind should be enough to incite the desire for change, but there is, in addition to all this, a factor we have barely touched on here: this capitalist industrial civilization is also killing the planet.[5] This is not a question of opinion but of fact, and a fact that impinges as much on the ruling classes as on the rest of the population. The situation could hardly be more urgent and yet our culture barely responds, shows no sign of changing. The core problem is perhaps that our society is no longer alive and you can't expect much in the way of response from a corpse! Our so-called democracy is a sham, the people disempowered and cowed into submission by Authority and there is therefore no obvious way that the majority can influence the direction society takes, even on detailed points, let alone issues of fundamental importance.

However, it is important to remember that this sensation of powerlessness is all part of the psychological trickery used by the authorities to ensure our compliance with the continuing status quo. Living collectively in the Now, we are blinded not only to the past, but to the future. More specifically, we have become convinced that just as Progress has inevitably brought us to where we are today, so it must continue to take us to wherever it must lead. We are taught that the future is essentially pre-determined, according to the historical laws which we are told have shaped our world, and there is nothing we can do about it. This lie has even come to be accepted by radical opponents of industrial capitalism, who insist that the best we can do is to adapt to the grim future that will inevitably be delivered to us by the system.

In truth, there was nothing inevitable about the way our society has turned out. As we have seen, it has taken centuries of repression to impose the will of a sociopathic elite on the population. That repression continues today, along with the possibility that it will fail to hold us down. Seen from our enemies' point of view, there is nothing inevitable about the continuation of their system at all. They live in constant fear of losing control, of being overwhelmed by the sheer numbers of the lawless mob. That is why they devote so much time and energy to feeding us lies, locking us up, acting out the theatre of Authority, sending in riot cops and armies to put down any signs of resistance to their global slave-labour system.

We are living in an age when many of the illusions of Authority are falling away and many millions of people across the world are seeing the truth behind the false constructs which prop it up. Cynicism is rife but we seem to have stopped there, balanced on the point of no longer believing in the system but unwilling to go any further, to take the final step into outright resistance. Now is the moment for us to explode the ultimate lie with which we have been brainwashed – that we are powerless.

The first step is to understand how it is that we have been duped, how the concepts of Authority, divine and temporal, have been combined to reduce us to a state of psychological submission. Then we have to rediscover within ourselves the vital spirit that makes us strong, the sense of collective belonging and empowerment that so frightens those who would keep us and our descendants as their slaves. It barely matters what we term this power within, so long as we do not allow it to be overshadowed by the myth of a power outside or above us – there can be no authority, no god, but ourselves.

Although this is just the first step, it is also the most important, as everything else will flow from this realisation, this absolute rejection of the "sense of nullity or of unworthiness" that Robin Zaehner so helpfully identified as crucial for a passively obedient population. "Modifying the mental outlook of a people is the one and only means of bringing about any deep or lasting change",[6] observes René Guénon, and there can be no more fundamental modification of a people's mental outlook than this one.

From this new perspective, or rather old perspective rediscovered, the situation of the human race looks quite different. It seems impossible that it could ever bow its head in slavery or stand idly by while its mother, the Earth, is destroyed in the name of short-term greed. It seems unthinkable that people could ever have forgotten that the desire for freedom lies at the heart of their very being. Reconnected with the long-forbidden knowledge of their own power, a people will naturally be propelled towards its innate and eternal needs.

Idries Shah writes that "it is maintained by Sufis that even in cultures where authoritarian and mechanical thinking have choked comprehensive understanding, human individuality will have to assert itself, somewhere, even if this be only through the primitive sense that life must have more meaning than the officially propagated one".[7] Like the green shoots of a plant seeking out the sunlight, humanity will always have a natural tendency to fulfil its inner organic potential.

Roger N. Baldwin notes that Kropotkin often pointed out that anarchism "is only the formulation of a universal and ancient desire of mankind",[8] and Kropotkin could be describing our own times when he argues that "there are periods in the life of human society when revolution becomes an imperative necessity, when it proclaims itself as inevitable".[9] But, of course, revolution is only inevitable, or indeed possible, if we take whatever action is necessary to bring it about.

It is here that we must again confront the comfortable habit of perpetually living in the Now and with it the whole concept of time as something that sweeps us along like small twigs in a surging river. This is Time regarded as Authority, as an obstacle to our power to shape our own reality, to become the people we want to be. We are not bound to travel to any particular future, there is nothing inevitable about any outcome, no matter how likely it may look from our present vantage point. While we recognise the existence of circumstances that stand in the way of the future we would like to see, there is no reason why we must therefore accept that their influence will be decisive. It is, as Ernst Bloch says, always possible to replace the fatalism of a "because" with the determination of a "despite everything".[10]

We have to reintroduce ourselves to history, not as observers but as participants. The power that we can rediscover in ourselves is, among other things, the power to create the future. We have to create our own axis in time, our own narrative – the narrative of revolution. Like the prophesies of the English Revolutionaries or the Camisards, our narrative can become self-fulfilling. There is a self-feeding circular momentum that we need to get started. The understanding of the need for revolution, the dream of revolution, the hope of revolution, the belief in the possibility of revolution – all of these must be fostered in turn before revolution can ever take place.

For this task we need a powerful collective vision and determination that can inspire, that can transform, that can regenerate, that can sweep aside seemingly immovable obstacles and turn remote possibilities into hard realities. Humankind needs new generations of idealistic young revolutionaries, heretics, *inspirés* with a burning sense of purpose and destiny, with the unquenchable energy to *will* into existence the new world of which they dream. We need, as Kropotkin insists, "intrepid souls who know that is necessary to *dare* in order to succeed".[11]

We won't get them by sticking to dry dispassionate analysis of history, by being bogged down in detail, by being waylaid into dead ends of pointless abstraction or pedantry. We won't get them by shying away from the truth, by compromising with the system, by regarding passionate polemic as an embarrassment. We won't get them by trying to regulate and repress the spirit of our own revolt, by pouring cold water on others' attempts to bring about change, by sneering at hope itself.

There are those who reject hope as unrealistic and those who reject it as being passive, as being reliant on factors outside our own control. But both positions fail to see that hope is in fact a vital factor in our ability to change reality and that, far from playing a passive role, it is the key to inspiring active participation. "Let us remember that if exasperation often drives men to revolt, it is always hope, the hope of victory, which makes revolutions",[12] says Kropotkin and he argues that the action it inspires will itself feed back into the positive energies of the revolutionary spirit: "Courage, devotion, the spirit of sacrifice, are as contagious as cowardice, submission, and panic".[13] Prophecy brings hope, hope brings courage, courage brings action, action brings inspiration, inspiration brings more determination, renewed hope, deepened courage. Once this magical spiral of revolt has started spinning, it takes on a life of its own and becomes, in Kropotkin's phrase, "a revolutionary whirlwind".[14]

The authentic urge to revolution can be destructive, but never negative, and behind it there be must always be a vision born from the heart of humanity. Gustav Landauer writes: "In unspiritual times of decline, un-culture, un-spirit, and misery, men who suffer not only externally but also internally under this general condition which seeks to engulf them fully – in their life, thought, feeling and will – men who resist this engulfment must have an ideal".[15] A common theme among the rebels we have discussed here has been the belief in a past Golden Age to which they hoped humankind would return. As Yves Delhoysie argues: "It's not relevant here to discuss whether the Golden Age existed at one point, somewhere. The real question is rather that people have always been fascinated by the idea of a time and a world where everyone lived in complete freedom, without being subjugated into labour and without being divided by the rule of money and private property".[16]

There is something therefore much deeper behind the will to genuine revolution, to anarchy, than mere opinion. It rises from the depths of our collective soul and thus, by extension, from the natural world of which we are part. It is the vehicle of an intangible organic need for things to be made right, for humankind and the planet it dominates to once again exist in harmony with the Tao. This restoration of the state of nature, of the Golden Age, is demanded by natural laws next to which our artificial human laws look feeble and ephemeral. Once unleashed, the mighty strength of a global uprising summoned by the life-force itself will have no difficulty in sweeping away for ever the violent machineries of a tyranny which has stifled humankind for far too long.

ENDNOTES

I

The Dispossessed

1. Parra-Wa-Samen (Ten Bears) of the Yamparika Comanches, cit. Dee Brown, *Bury My Heart at Wounded Knee: An Indian History of the American West,* (London: Vintage, 1991) p. 242.
2. Brown, p. 3.
3. Christopher Hill, *The World Turned Upside Down: Radical Ideas During the English Revolution,* (London: Pelican, 1975) pp. 132-33.
4. Hill, p. 133.
5. E.P. Thompson, *Customs in Common,* (London: Penguin, 1993) p. 125.
6. John Prebble, *The Highland Clearances,* (London: Penguin, 1976) p. 258.
7. Thompson, p. 134.
8. Thompson, p. 135.
9. The Office of Woods and Forests, Land Revenue, Works and Buildings, *Law Magazine and Quarterly Review of Jurisprudence,* n.s. 14/o.s 45 (1851) pp. 31-33. cit. Thompson, p. 107.
10. Thompson, p. 164.
11. Thompson, p. 280.
12. Brown, p. 376.
13. Brown, p. 388.
14. S. Fortrey, *Englands Interest and Improvement,* (1663) pp. 19-20, cit. Hill, p. 51.
15. Hill, p. 53.
16. Hill, p. 43.
17. Thompson, p. 141.
18. Yves Delhoysie, *Le millénarisme et la chute du monde Chrétien*, in Yves Delhoysie & Georges Lapierre, *L'Incendie millénariste,* (Paris: Os Cangaceiros, 2011) p. 72.
19. Thompson, p. 221.
20. Hill, p. 349.

21. Brown, p. 374.

22. Ibid.

23. *Les Amis de Ludd: Bulletin d'information anti-industriel* (*Los Amigos de Ludd. Boletín de información anti-industriel*), numéros un à quatre, (Paris: Petite capitale, 2005) p. 95.

24. Peter Kropotkin, *Anarchist Communism: Its Basis and Principles*, in *Kropotkin's Revolutionary Pamphlets: A Collection of Writings by Peter Kropotkin*, ed. by Roger N. Baldwin, (New York: Dover Publications, 1970) p. 55.

25. Kropotkin, *Anarchism: Its Philosophy and Ideal*, in *Kropotkin's Revolutionary Pamphlets*, p. 128.

26. Gustav Landauer, *For Socialism*, trans. by David J Parent, (St Louis: Telos Press, 1978) p. 128.

27. William Morris, *Useful Work Versus Useless Toil* (1885) in *News From Nowhere and Selected Writings and Designs*, ed. by Asa Briggs, (London: Penguin, 1984) p. 119.

28. Morris, *Useful Work Versus Useless Toil*, in *News From Nowhere*, p. 117.

29. Thompson, p. 167.

30. Erich Fromm, *Zur Psychologie des Verbrechers und der strafenden Gesellschaft*, Imago, Band XVIII, 1931, pp. 247-49, cit. Michael Löwy, *Rédemption et utopie: le judaïsme libertaire en Europe centrale*, (Paris: Éditions du Sandre, 2009) p. 192.

31. Thompson, p. 43.

32. Thompson, p. 45.

33. Thompson, p. 46.

34. Kropotkin, *Law and Authority*, in *Kropotkin's Revolutionary Pamphlets*, p. 211.

35. Kropotkin, *Law and Authority*, in *Kropotkin's Revolutionary Pamphlets*, p. 207.

36. Prebble, p. 44.

37. Prebble, p. 36.

38. Prebble, p. 238.

39. Franz Kafka, *The Trial* and *Metamorphosis*, (London: Landmark, 1983) p. 159.

40. Löwy, *Rédemption et utopie*, p. 99.

41. Kropotkin, *Modern Science and Anarchism* in *Kropotkin's Revolutionary Pamphlets*, p. 183.

42. Friedrich Nietzsche, *Thus Spoke Zarathustra: A Book for Everyone and No One*, trans. by RJ Hollingdale, (London: Penguin, 1977) p. 76.

43. Tom Anderson, *When Co-Option Fails* in *Managing Democracy, Managing Dissent: Capitalism, Democracy and the Organisation of Consent*, ed. by Rebecca Fisher, (London: Corporate Watch, 2013) pp. 232-33.

44. Prebble, p. 50.

45. Prebble, p. 45.

46. Prebble, p. 79.
47. Prebble, p. 231.
48. Michael Bakunin, *The Bear of Berne and the Bear of St Petersburg* in *The Political Philosophy of Bakunin: Scientific Anarchism*, ed. by G.P. Maximoff, (New York: The Free Press of Glencoe, 1964) p. 140.

II

Cultural Resistance

1. Ian MacCodrum, cit. John Prebble, *The Highland Clearances*, (London: Penguin, 1976) p. 20.
2. E.P. Thompson, *Customs in Common*, (London: Penguin, 1993) p. 184.
3. Christopher Hill, *The World Turned Upside Down: Radical Ideas During the English Revolution*, (London: Pelican, 1975) p. 53.
4. Paul Cudenec, *The Anarchist Revelation: Being What We're Meant to Be*, (Sussex: Winter Oak, 2013) p. 23.
5. Prebble, p. 15.
6. Thompson, p. 182.
7. Keith Thomas, *Religion and the Decline of Magic*, (London: Penguin, 1991) p. 75.
8. Chris Hare, *Worthing, a History: Riot and Respectability in a Seaside Town*, (Chichester, Phillimore, 2008) p. 11.
9. Hare, p. 22.
10. John MacCulloch, *The Highlands and Western Islands of Scotland*, (1824) cit. Prebble, pp. 150-51.
11. Mircea Eliade, *Myths, Dreams and Mysteries: The Encounter Between Contemporary Faiths and Archaic Reality*, trans. by Philip Mairet, (London: Collins, 1974) p. 165.
12. Ibid.
13. Heinmot Tooyalaket (Chief Joseph) of the Nez Percés, cit. Dee Brown, *Bury My Heart at Wounded Knee: An Indian History of the American West*, (London: Vintage, 1991) p. 316.
14. Thompson, p. 179.
15. Peter Kropotkin, *Law and Authority*, in *Kropotkin's Revolutionary Pamphlets: A Collection of Writings by Peter Kropotkin*, ed. by Roger N. Baldwin, (New York: Dover Publications, 1970) p. 201.
16. Kropotkin, *Law and Authority*, in *Kropotkin's Revolutionary Pamphlets*, p. 202.
17. Herbert Read, *The Forms of Things Unknown: Essays Towards An Aesthetic Philosophy*, (New York: Horizon Press, 1960) pp. 95-96.
18. Thompson, p. 164.
19. Thompson, p. 188.

20. Thompson, p. 9.
21. Thompson, p. 520.
22. Thompson, pp. 521-22.
23. Kropotkin, *Anarchism: Its Philosophy and Ideal*, in *Kropotkin's Revolutionary Pamphlets*, pp. 131-32.
24. James Loch, cit. Prebble, p. 56.
25. John Robertson, cit. Prebble, p. 209.
26. Loch, cit. Prebble, p. 69.
27. Prebble, p. 70.
28. Brown, p. 2.
29. Henry Sewell in *New Zealand Parliamentary Debates*, 9 (1870) p. 361, cit. Thompson, p. 166.

III

Underground Freedom

1. Joseph Campbell, *The Masks of God: Creative Mythology*, (London: Penguin, 1976) p. 629.
2. Yves Delhoysie, *Le millénarisme et la chute du monde Chrétien*, in Yves Delhoysie & Georges Lapierre, *L'Incendie millénariste*, (Paris: Os Cangaceiros, 2011) p. 48.
3. Campbell, p. 406.
4. Campbell, p. 169.
5. Adrian G Gilbert, *Foreword, Hermetica: The Ancient Greek and Latin Writings Which Contain Religious or Philosophic Teachings Ascribed to Hermes Trismegistus*, (Shaftesbury: Solos Press, 1997) pp. 7-8.
6. Campbell, p. 400.
7. Delhoysie, *Le millénarisme et la chute du monde Chrétien* in *L'Incendie millénariste*, p. 59.
8. Philippe Joutard, *Les Camisards*, (Paris: Gallimard/Julliard, 1976) p. 22.
9. Robert Graves, *Introduction*, Idries Shah, *The Sufis*, (London: WH Allen & Co, 1977) p. xiii.
10. See also Paul Cudenec, *The Anarchist Revelation: Being What We're Meant to Be*, (Sussex: Winter Oak, 2013) pp. 89-93.
11. Shah, p. 356.
12. Lynn Picknett & Clive Prince, *The Templar Revelation: Secret Guardians of the True Identity of Christ*, (London: Corgi, 1998) p. 419.
13. Picknett & Prince, p. 115.
14. Graves, *Introduction*, Shah, p. x.
15. Graves, *Introduction*, Shah, p. xi.
16. Graves says the name "troubador" comes from the Arabic root TRB, meaning "lutanist". Graves, *Introduction*, Shah, p. xiv.

17. The coat of arms of the order's founder, Hugue de Payns ("of the Pagans"), who was born in 1070, was three Saracen heads sable, "blazoned as if cut off in battle, but really denoting heads of wisdom". Graves, *Introduction*, Shah, p. xix.

18. Graves, *Introduction*, Shah, pp. xix-xx.

19. Graves, *Introduction*, Shah, p. xix.

20. "It is a play on two Arabic roots FHM and FHHM, pronounced *fecham* and *facham*, one of which means 'black' and the other 'wise'". Graves, *Introduction*, Shah, p. xix.

21. Shah, p. xxv.

22. Graves, *Introduction*, Shah, pp. xx-xxi.

23. Graves, *Introduction*, Shah, p. xxi.

24. Georges Lapierre, *Introduction au millénarisme* in *L'Incendie millénariste*, p. 35.

25. Picknett & Prince, pp. 175-6.

26. Lapierre, *Épilogue*, in *L'Incendie millénariste*, p. 146.

27. Delhoysie, *Le millénarisme et la chute du monde Chrétien*, in *L'Incendie millénariste*, p. 61.

29. Raoul Vaneigem, *Les Hérésies* (Paris: *Que sais-je?*, Presses Universitaires de France) p. 94.

29. Delhoysie, *Le millénarisme et la chute du monde Chrétien*, in *L'Incendie millénariste*, p. 67.

30. Jan van Ruysbroeck, cit. Delhoysie, *Le millénarisme et la chute du monde Chrétien*, in *L'Incendie millénariste*, p. 68.

31. Raoul Vaneigem, *Frères du libre-esprit, Dossier: Avant la révolution, Offensive: trimestriel d'offensive libertaire et sociale*, No 28, Dec 2010.

32. Lapierre, *Épilogue*, in *L'Incendie millénariste*, p. 147.

33. Delhoysie, *Le millénarisme et la chute du monde Chrétien*, in *L'Incendie millénariste*, p. 96.

34. Delhoysie, *Le millénarisme et la chute du monde Chrétien*, in *L'Incendie millénariste*, p. 102.

35. Delhoysie, *Le millénarisme et la chute du monde Chrétien*, in *L'Incendie millénariste*, p. 104.

36. Ibid.

37. Delhoysie, *Le millénarisme et la chute du monde Chrétien*, in *L'Incendie millénariste*, p. 85.

IV

Disenchanted Lives

1. Keith Thomas, *Religion and the Decline of Magic*, (London: Penguin, 1991) p. 54.
2. Ibid.
3. Thomas, p. 257.
4. Thomas, pp. 301-02.
5. Thomas, p. 292.
6. Thomas, p. 535.
7. Colin Wilson, *The Occult*, (London: Granada, 1981) p. 279.
8. Adrian G Gilbert, *Foreword, Hermetica: The Ancient Greek and Latin Writings Which Contain Religious or Philosophic Teachings Ascribed to Hermes Trismegistus,* (Shaftesbury: Solos Press, 1997) pp. 6-7.
9. Alan Watts, *The Book On the Taboo Against Knowing Who You Are,* (London: Souvenir, 2012) p. 115.
10. *La France Occulte: L'étonnant retour des druides, sorciers, médiums et autres guérisseurs* in *Le Figaro Magazine,* (Paris: November 1, 2013) pp. 44-52.
11. Thomas, p. 765.
12. René Guénon, *Introduction to the Study of the Hindu Doctrines*, trans. by Marco Pallis, (Hillsdale, NY: Sophia Perennis, 2004) p. 108.
13. *La France Occulte* in *Le Figaro Magazine,* p. 51.
14. Thomas, p. 512.

V

From Prophets to Profits

1. Yves Delhoysie, *Le millénarisme et la chute du monde Chrétien*, in Yves Delhoysie & Georges Lapierre, *L'Incendie millénariste,* (Paris: Os Cangaceiros, 2011) p. 106.
2. Ernst Bloch, *Thomas Münzer, théologien de la révolution*, trans. by Maurice de Gandillac, (Paris: Les Prairies ordinaires, 2012) p. 212.
3. Georges Lapierre, *Introduction au millénarisme*, in *L'Incendie millénariste,* p. 28.
4. Delhoysie, *Le millénarisme et la chute du monde Chrétien*, in *L'Incendie millénariste,* p. 129.
5. Bloch, p. 294.
6. Lapierre, *Les révoltés de Münster*, in *L'Incendie millénariste,* p. 142.
7. Christopher Hill, *The World Turned Upside Down: Radical Ideas During the English Revolution,* (London: Pelican, 1975) p. 26.

8. Hill, p. 27.
9. Lapierre, *Introduction au millénarisme*, in *L'Incendie millénariste*, p. 33.
10. Hill, p. 29.
11. Hill, p. 14.
12. Peter Marshall, *Demanding the Impossible: A History of Anarchism*, (London: Fontana Press, 1993) p. 96.
13. Bloch, p. 140.
14. Bloch, p. 137.
15. Gérard de Sède, *700 ans de révoltes occitanes,* (Paris: Plon, 1982) p. 113.
16. Philippe Joutard, *Les Camisards,* (Paris: Gallimard/Julliard, 1976) pp. 86-87.
17. Hill, p. 91.
18. Bloch, p. 108.
19. Delhoysie, *Le millénarisme et la chute du monde Chrétien*, in *L'Incendie millénariste*, p. 132.
20. Hill, p. 90.
21. Hill, p. 89.
22. Hill, p. 361.
23. Keith Thomas, *Religion and the Decline of Magic,* (London: Penguin, 1991) p. 177.
24. Thomas, p. 178.
25. Joutard, p. 70.
26. Joutard, p. 88.
27. Joutard, p. 150.
28. Joutard, p. 113.
29. Joutard, p. 86.
30. Durand Fage, cit. Joutard, p. 153.
31. Joutard, p. 87.
32. Hill, p. 89.
33. Hill, p. 291.
34. Hill, p. 290.
35. Hill, p. 363.
36. Bloch, p. 96.
37. Bloch, p. 89.
38. Lynn Picknett & Clive Prince, *The Templar Revelation: Secret Guardians of the True Identity of Christ,* (London: Corgi, 1998) p. 115.
39. Richard Coppin, *Divine Teachings,* (2nd edn, 1653) pp. 8-10, cit. Hill, pp. 220-21.
40. Hill, p. 219.
41. Hill, p. 206.
42. Gerrard Winstanley, *The Law of Freedom*, cit. Hill, p. 142.
43. Bloch, p. 270.
44. Lapierre, *Les révoltés de Münster*, in *L'Incendie millénariste,* p. 139.
45. Hill, p. 206.

46. Ibid.

47. See, for instance, Clifford Harper, *Anarchy: A Graphic Guide,* (London: Camden Press, 1987) or Marshall, *Demanding the Impossible.*

48. Gustav Landauer, *Beginnen: Aufsätze über Sozialismus,* ed. by Martin Buber, Cologne, 1924, p. 16, cit. Charles B Maurer, *Call to Revolution. The Mystical Anarchism of Gustav Landauer,* (Detroit: Wayne State University Press, 1971) p. 92.

49. Hill, p. 149.

50. Hill, p. 14.

51. Thomas, p. 178.

52. Gerald Bullett, *The English Mystics,* (London: Michael Joseph, 1950) p. 72.

53. Hill, p. 382.

54. Peter Marshall, *William Blake: Visionary Anarchist,* (London: Freedom Press, 2008) p. 21.

55. Marshall, *William Blake,* p. 22.

56. Ibid.

57. Hill, p. 161.

58. Bloch, p. 213.

59. Delhoysie, *Le millénarisme et la chute du monde Chrétien,* in *L'Incendie millénariste,* p. 129.

60. Bloch, p. 66.

61. Gustav Landauer, *Revolution and Other Writings: A Political Reader,* ed. and trans. by Gabriel Kuhn, (Oakland: PM Press, 2010) p. 142.

62. Bloch, p. 167.

63. John Prebble, *The Highland Clearances,* (London: Penguin, 1976) p. 127.

64. Delhoysie, *Le millénarisme et la chute du monde Chrétien,* in *L'Incendie millénariste,* p. 107.

65. Thomas, p. 74.

66. Thomas, pp. 74-75.

67. Rupert Sheldrake, *The Rebirth of Nature: The Greening of Science and God,* (London: Rider, 1991) p. 19.

68. George Woodcock, *Anarchism,* (London: Penguin, 1979) p. 40.

69. Joutard, p. 20.

70. Joutard, p. 44.

71. Sheldrake, p. 20.

72. Sheldrake, pp. 20-21.

73. Hill, pp. 294-95.

74. Hill, p. 296.

75. Hill, p. 297.

76. Bloch, p. 140.

77. De Sède, pp. 113-14.

78. Delhoysie, *Le millénarisme et la chute du monde Chrétien,* in *L'Incendie millénariste,* p. 136.

79. Delhoysie, *Le millénarisme et la chute du monde Chrétien*, in *L'Incendie millénariste*, p. 107.

80. Delhoysie, *Le millénarisme et la chute du monde Chrétien*, in *L'Incendie millénariste*, p. 135.

81. Hill, p. 15.

82. Bloch, p. 182.

83. Thomas, p. 90.

84. Hill, p. 388.

85. Hill, p. 157.

86. Delhoysie, *Le millénarisme et la chute du monde Chrétien*, in *L'Incendie millénariste*, p. 136.

87. Landauer, *Revolution*, p. 142.

88. René Guénon, *Introduction to the Study of the Hindu Doctrines*, trans. by Marco Pallis, (Hillsdale, NY: Sophia Perennis, 2004) p. 232.

VI

Creative Block

1. Ananada K Coomaraswamy, *The Transformation of Nature in Art,* (New York: Dover, 1956) p. 9.

2. Herbert Read, *The Forms of Things Unknown: Essays Towards An Aesthetic Philosophy,* (New York: Horizon Press, 1960) p. 232.

3. Read, p. 105.

4. William Morris, *The Lesser Arts* (1878) in *News From Nowhere and Selected Writings and Designs*, ed. by Asa Briggs, (London: Penguin, 1984) p. 89.

5. Morris, *The Lesser Arts* in *News From Nowhere*, p. 93.

6. Morris, *Useful Work Versus Useless Toil* (1885) in *News From Nowhere*, pp. 133-34.

7. A. Holitscher, *Amerika heute und morgen,* (Berlin: Fischer-Verlag, 1912) p. 316, cit. Michael Löwy, *Rédemption et utopie: le judaïsme libertaire en Europe centrale,* (Paris: Éditions du Sandre, 2009) p. 95.

8. G. Janouch, *Gespräche mit Kafka,* (Frankfurt: Fischer Verlag, 1968) p. 159, cit. Löwy, p. 95.

9. Morris, *The Lesser Arts,* in *News From Nowhere*, p. 89.

10. Coomaraswamy, p. 37.

11. Coomaraswamy, p. 65.

12. Ibid.

13. Coomaraswamy, pp. 40-42.

14. Morris, *The Lesser Arts* in *News From Nowhere*, p. 85.

15. Morris, *Some Hints on Pattern Designing* (1881 lecture at Working Men's College, London) in *News From Nowhere*, p. 106.

16. Morris, *The Worker's Share of Art* (1885) in *News From Nowhere*, p. 142.

17. Coomaraswamy, p. 25.

18. Walter Benjamin, *Illuminations*, ed. by Hannah Arendt, trans. by Harry Zohn, (London: Jonathan Cape, 1970) p. 223.

19. Gerald Bullett, *The English Mystics*, (London: Michael Joseph, 1950) p. 174.

20. Read, p. 27.

21. Read, p. 75.

22. Morris, *The Lesser Arts* in *News From Nowhere*, p. 85.

23. William Blake, *Blake: Complete Writings*, ed. by Geoffrey Keynes, Oxford University Press, 1972, p. 459, cit. Peter Marshall, *William Blake: Visionary Anarchist*, (London: Freedom Press, 2008) p. 30.

24. Marshall, p. 30.

25. Morris, *The Lesser Arts* in *News From Nowhere*, p. 87.

26. Joseph Campbell, *The Masks of God: Creative Mythology*, (London: Penguin, 1976) p. 94.

27. Read, p. 51.

28. Read, p. 61.

29. Read, p. 63.

30. Ibid.

31. Morris, *How I Became A Socialist*, in *News From Nowhere*, p. 36.

32. René Guénon, *The Reign of Quantity and the Signs of the Times*, trans. by Lord Northbourne, (Hillsdale, NY: Sophia Perennis, 2004) p. 192.

33. Read, p. 12.

34. Ernst Bloch, *Geist der Utopie* (1923 version), (Frankfurt: Suhrkamp, 1973) pp. 20-21, cit. Löwy, p. 175.

VII

Romantic Revolutionaries

1. Paul Cudenec, *The Anarchist Revelation: Being What We're Meant to Be*, (Sussex: Winter Oak, 2013) pp. 48-51.

2. René Guénon, *East and West*, trans. by Martin Lings, (Hillsdale, NY: Sophia Perennis, 2004) p. 38.

3. René Guénon, *Introduction to the Study of the Hindu Doctrines*, (Hillsdale, NY: Sophia Perennis, 2004) p. 216.

4. Guénon, *Introduction to the Study of the Hindu Doctrines*, p. 215.

5. Herbert Read, *The Forms of Things Unknown: Essays Towards An Aesthetic Philosophy*, (New York: Horizon Press, 1960) p. 16.

6. Alan Watts, *The Book On the Taboo Against Knowing Who You Are*, (London: Souvenir, 2012) pp. 146-47.

7. Friedrich Nietzsche, *Twilight of the Idols and The Anti-Christ*, trans. by RJ Hollingdale, (London: Penguin, 1968) p. 62.

8. Richard Noll, *The Jung Cult: The Origins of a Charismatic Movement*,

(London: Fontana, 1996) pp. 28-29.

9. Noll, p. 29.

10. Noll, p. 49.

11. Noll, p. 101.

12. Hanz Kohn, *Martin Buber*, 1930, pp. 60-65, cit. Michael Löwy, *Rédemption et utopie: le judaïsme libertaire en Europe centrale*, (Paris: Éditions du Sandre, 2009) p. 200.

13. Löwy, *Rédemption et utopie*, p. 40.

14. Löwy, *Rédemption et utopie*, pp. 40-41.

15. Löwy, *Rédemption et utopie*, p. 222.

16. George Woodcock, *Anarchism*, (London: Penguin, 1979) p. 286.

17. Löwy, *Rédemption et utopie*, p. 226.

18. Michael Löwy, *Juifs hétérdoxes: Romantisme, messianisme, utopie*, (Paris: Éditions de l' éclat; 2010) p. 83.

19. R.C. Zaehner, *Mysticism Sacred and Profane: An Inquiry Into some Varieties of Praeternatural Experience*, (Oxford: Oxford University Press, 1971) p. 45.

20. Gerald Bullett, *The English Mystics*, (London: Michael Joseph, 1950) p. 22.

21. Richard Jefferies, *The Story of My Heart: My Autobiography*, (London: Quartet, 1979) p. 57.

22. William Morris, *How I Became A Socialist*, in *News From Nowhere and Selected Writings and Designs*, ed. by Asa Briggs, (London: Penguin, 1984) p. 36.

23. Bullett, p. 186.

24. Peter Marshall, *William Blake: Visionary Anarchist*, (London: Freedom Press, 2008) p. 24.

25. Michael Bakunin, *Marxism, Freedom and the State*, trans. by K.J. Kenafick, (London: Freedom Press, 1990) p. 21.

26. Emma Goldman, *Living My Life,* Vol II, (London: Duckworth, 1932) p. 757.

27. Russell Berman & Tim Luke, *Introduction*, Gustav Landauer, *For Socialism*, trans. by David J Parent, (St Louis: Telos Press, 1978) p. 6.

28. Berman & Luke, *Introduction*, Landauer, p. 7.

29. Berman & Luke, *Introduction*, Landauer, p. 11.

30. Berman & Luke, *Introduction*, Landauer, p. 10.

31. Berman & Luke, *Introduction*, Landauer, p. 11.

32. Landauer, p. 32.

33. Landauer, p. 46.

34. Landauer, p. 55.

35. Landauer, p. 123.

36. Landauer, p. 56.

37. Landauer, p. 109.

38. Ernst Bloch, *Thomas Münzer, théologien de la révolution*, trans. by

Maurice de Gandillac, (Paris: Les Prairies ordinaires, 2012) pp. 88-89.
39. Goldman, Vol I, p. 9.
40. Goldman, Vol I, p. 56.
41. Bakunin, p. 50.
42. Landauer, p. 57.
43. Landauer, p. 82.
44. http://theanarchistlibrary.org/library/Various_Authors__
Reply_by_several_Russian_Anarchists_to_the__Platform_.html
45. Landauer, p. 134.

VIII

The World Soul

1. Richard Noll, *The Jung Cult: The Origins of a Charismatic Movement,* (London: Fontana, 1996) p. 104.
2. Noll, p. 175.
3. Noll, p. 237.
4. Noll, p. 42.
5. Emma Goldman, *Living My Life*, Vol II, (London: Duckworth, 1932) p. 695.
6. Goldman, Vol II, p. 709.
7. Russell Berman & Tim Luke, *Introduction*, Gustav Landauer, *For Socialism*, trans. by David J Parent, (St Louis: Telos Press, 1978) p. 8.
8. Berman & Luke, *Introduction*, Landauer, p. 3.
9. Berman & Luke, *Introduction*, Landauer, p. 8.
10. Ibid.
11. Landauer, p. 34.
12. Noll, p. 76.
13. Noll, p. 108.
14. Michael Löwy, *Rédemption et utopie: le judaïsme libertaire en Europe centrale,* (Paris: Éditions du Sandre, 2009) p. 109.
15. Walter Benjamin, *Illuminations*, ed. by Hannah Arendt, trans. by Harry Zohn, (London: Jonathan Cape, 1970) p. 134.
16. Löwy, *Rédemption et utopie*, p. 107.
17. Ibid.
18. Löwy, *Rédemption et utopie*, p. 94.
19. Löwy, *Rédemption et utopie*, p. 8.
20. Löwy, *Rédemption et utopie*, p. 13.
21. Löwy, *Rédemption et utopie*, p. 8.
22. Michael Löwy, *Juifs hétérdoxes: Romantisme, messianisme, utopie,* (Paris: Éditions de l' éclat; 2010) p. 22.
23. Ernst Toller, *Eine Jugend in Deutschland* (1933), Carl Hanser Verlag, 1978, pp. 227-28, cit. Löwy, *Rédemption et utopie*, p. 213.
24. Bernard Lazare: *La Question Juive*, (Paris: Editions Allia, 2012) p. 12.

25. Löwy, *Rédemption et utopie*, p. 26.

26. Löwy, *Rédemption et utopie*, p. 167.

27. Löwy, *Rédemption et utopie*, p. 27.

28. Ernst Bloch, *Thomas Münzer, théologien de la révolution*, trans. by Maurice de Gandillac, (Paris: Les Prairies ordinaires, 2012) pp. 298-99.

29. Thierry Labica, *Un contretemps nommé Thomas Münzer*, Bloch, p. 17.

30. Michael Löwy, *Walter Benjamin et le surréalisme* in *Europe: revue littéraire mensuelle, Walter Benjamin*, avril 1996, p. 83.

31. Löwy, *Rédemption et utopie*, p. 148.

32. Löwy, *Juifs hétérdoxes*, p. 36.

33. Löwy, *Rédemption et utopie*, p. 34.

34. Ibid.

35. Landauer, p. 102.

36. Frank McLynn, *Carl Gustav Jung*, (New York: St Martin's Griffin, 1998) p. 511.

37. Herbert Read, *The Forms of Things Unknown: Essays Towards An Aesthetic Philosophy*, (New York: Horizon Press, 1960) pp. 189-90.

38. Noll, p. 274.

39. Mark Sedgwick, *Against The Modern World: Traditionalism and the Secret Intellectual History of the Twentieth Century*, (New York: Oxford University Press, 2009) p. 29.

40. René Guénon, *The Crisis of the Modern World*, trans. by Arthur Osborne, Marco Pallis & Richard C Nicholson, (Ghent, NY: Sophia Perennis, 2001) p. 17.

41. René Guénon, *Introduction to the Study of the Hindu Doctrines*, trans. by Marco Pallis, (Hillsdale, NY: Sophia Perennis, 2004) p. 22.

42. Guénon, *Introduction to the Study of the Hindu Doctrines*, p. 249.

43. Guénon, *The Crisis of the Modern World*, p. 98.

44. See Paul Cudenec, *The Anarchist Revelation: Being What We're Meant to Be*, (Sussex: Winter Oak, 2013) pp. 81-82.

45. Sedgwick, p. 187.

46. Noll, p. 103.

47. McLynn, p. 289.

48. McLynn, p. 276.

49. June Singer, *Boundaries of the Soul: The Practice of Jung's Psychology*, (New York: Anchor Books, 1989) p. xxiii.

50. Noll, p. 7.

51. Noll, p. 143.

52. Noll, p. 8.

IX

Total Rejection

1. Richard Noll, *The Jung Cult: The Origins of a Charismatic Movement*, (London: Fontana, 1996) p. 294.
2. Aldous Huxley, *The Perennial Philosophy*, (London: Chatto & Windus, 1980) p. 288.
3. Huxley, *The Perennial Philosophy*, p. 197.
4. Huxley, *The Perennial Philosophy*, p. 229.
5. Aldous Huxley, *Brave New World Revisited*, (London: Chatto and Windus, 1959) p. 17.
6. Huxley, *Brave New World Revisited*, p. 34.
7. Huxley, *Brave New World Revisited*, p. 35.
8. Huxley, *Brave New World Revisited*, p. 154.
9. Huxley, *Brave New World Revisited*, p. 156.
10. Huxley, *Brave New World Revisited*, p. 159.
11. R.C. Zaehner, *Mysticism Sacred and Profane: An Inquiry Into some Varieties of Praeternatural Experience*, (Oxford: Oxford University Press, 1971) p. 28.
12. Aldous Huxley, *The Doors of Perception*, p. 49, cit. Zaehner, p. 15.
13. Zaehner, p. 15.
14. Zaehner, p. 16.
15. Zaehner, p. 17.
16. Zaehner, p. 106.
17. Zaehner, p. 51.
18. Zaehner, p. 186.
19. Zaehner, p. 185.
20. Zaehner, p. 117.
21. Zaehner, p. 138.
22. Zaehner, p. 87.
23. Zaehner, p. 188.
24. Richard Noll, *The Jung Cult: The Origins of a Charismatic Movement*, (London: Fontana, 1996) p. 218.
25. Noll, p. 219.
26. Noll, p. 269.
27. Zaehner, p. 65.
28. Zaehner, p. 106.
29. Zaehner, p. 109.
30. Zaehner, p. 111.
31. Zaehner, p. 121.
32. Zaehner, p. 141.
33. Zaehner, p. 33.
34. Zaehner, p. 145.

35. René Guénon, *Man and His Becoming According to the Vedānta*, trans. by Richard C Nicholson, (Hillsdale, NY: Sophia Perennis, 2004) p. 52.
36. Guénon, p. 73.
37. Fritjof Capra, *The Tao of Physics: An exploration of the parallels between modern physics and Eastern mysticism*, (London: Flamingo, 1992) p. 72.
38. Zaehner, p. 112.
39. Zaehner, p. 181.
40. Zaehner, p. 158.
41. Robert Fisk, *Another Fine Mess*,
http://www.informationclearinghouse.info/article4588.htm
42. Zaehner, p. 2.
43. Huxley, *Brave New World Revisited*, p. 164.
44. Zaehner, p. 142.

X

A Crime Against Humanity

1. Joseph Campbell, *The Masks of God: Creative Mythology*, (London: Penguin, 1976) p. 20.
2. Gerald Bullett, *The English Mystics*, (London: Michael Joseph, 1950) p. 68.
3. Campbell, p. 43.
4. Campbell, p. 60.
5. CG Jung, *Psychology and Alchemy*, (London: Routledge, 1989) p. 313.
6. Bullett, p. 45.
7. Bullett, p. 17.
8. Blessed Jan van Ruysbroeck, *The Spiritual Espousals*, trans. by Eric Colledge, (London: Faber and Faber, 1952) pp. 170-71. cit. R.C. Zaehner, *Mysticism Sacred and Profane: An Inquiry Into some Varieties of Praeternatural Experience*, (Oxford: Oxford University Press, 1971) p. 171.
9. Bullett, p. 115.
10. Alan Watts, *Tao: The Watercourse Way*, with the collaboration of Al Chung-Liang Huang, (London: Arkana, 1992) p. 76.
11. Keith Thomas, *Religion and the Decline of Magic*, (London: Penguin, 1991) p. 774.
12. Rebecca Fisher, *Introduction* in *Managing Democracy, Managing Dissent: Capitalism, Democracy and the Organisation of Consent*, ed. by Rebecca Fisher, (London: Corporate Watch, 2013) p. 4.
13. Campbell, p. 373.
14. Campbell, p. 388.
15. Campbell, pp. 5-6.
16. Mircea Eliade, *Myths, Dreams and Mysteries: The Encounter Between Contemporary Faiths and Archaic Reality*, trans. by Philip Mairet, (London: Collins, 1974) p. 106.

17. Pierre-Joseph Proudhon, *Philosophie de la Misère*, 1846, vol ii, p. 398, cit. Henri de Lubac, *The Un-Marxian Socialist: A Study of Proudhon*, trans. by Canon RE Scantlebury, (London: Sheed and Ward, 1948) p. 294.

18. Forrest Reid, *Following Darkness*, (London: Arnold, 1902) p. 42, cit. Zaehner, p. 41.

19. Alan Watts, *Does it Matter?*, (New York: Pantheon Books) p. 37, cit. Anne Bancroft, *Modern Mystics and Sages*, (London & St Albans: Paladin, 1978) p. 16.

20. Campbell, p. 428.

21. Bullett, p. 227-28.

22. Richard Noll, *The Jung Cult: The Origins of a Charismatic Movement*, (London: Fontana, 1996) p. 257.

XI

The Spiral of Hope

1. *Les Amis de Ludd: Bulletin d'information anti-industriel* (*Los Amigos de Ludd. Boletín de información anti-industriel)* numéros un à quatre, (Paris: Petite capitale, 2005) p. 96.

2. Herbert Read, *The Forms of Things Unknown: Essays Towards An Aesthetic Philosophy*, (New York: Horizon Press, 1960) p. 153.

3. Michael Löwy, *Rédemption et utopie: le judaïsme libertaire en Europe centrale*, (Paris: Éditions du Sandre, 2009) p. 249.

4. Walter Benjamin, *Illuminations*, ed. by Hannah Arendt, trans. by Harry Zohn, (London: Jonathan Cape, 1970) pp. 259-260.

5. See Paul Cudenec, *The Anarchist Revelation: Being What We're Meant to Be*, (Sussex: Winter Oak, 2013) pp. 27-37.

6. René Guénon, *Introduction to the Study of the Hindu Doctrines*, trans. by Marco Pallis, (Hillsdale, NY: Sophia Perennis, 2004) p. 250.

7. Idries Shah, *The Sufis*, (London: WH Allen & Co, 1977) p. xxv.

8. Roger N Baldwin, *Introduction, Kropotkin's Revolutionary Pamphlets: A Collection of Writings by Peter Kropotkin*, ed. by Roger N. Baldwin, (New York: Dover Publications, 1970) p. 11.

9. Peter Kropotkin, *The Spirit of Revolt*, in *Kropotkin's Revolutionary Pamphlets*, p. 35.

10. Ernst Bloch, *Thomas Münzer, théologien de la révolution*, trans. by Maurice de Gandillac, (Paris: Les Prairies ordinaires, 2012) p. 204.

11. Kropotkin, *The Spirit of Revolt* in *Kropotkin's Revolutionary Pamphlets*, p. 39.

12. Kropotkin, *The Spirit of Revolt* in *Kropotkin's Revolutionary Pamphlets*, p. 41.

13. Kropotkin, *The Spirit of Revolt* in *Kropotkin's Revolutionary Pamphlets*, p. 38.

14. Kropotkin, *The Spirit of Revolt* in *Kropotkin's Revolutionary Pamphlets*, p. 36.

15. Gustav Landauer, *For Socialism*, trans. by David J Parent, (St Louis: Telos Press, 1978) p. 29.

16. Yves Delhoysie, *Le millénarisme et la chute du monde Chrétien*, in Yves Delhoysie & Georges Lapierre, *L'Incendie millénariste*, (Paris: Os Cangaceiros, 2011) p. 64.

Also by Paul Cudenec

THE ANARCHIST REVELATION

Paul Cudenec draws on an impressively wide range of authors to depict a corrupted civilization on the brink of self-destruction and to call for a powerful new philosophy of resistance and renewal offering a future for humanity in which we are all able to "be what we're meant to be". He combines the anarchism of the likes of Gustav Landauer, Michael Bakunin and Herbert Read with the philosophy of René Guénon, Herbert Marcuse and Jean Baudrillard; the existentialism of Karl Jaspers and Colin Wilson; the vision of Carl Jung, Oswald Spengler and Idries Shah, and the environmental insight of Derrick Jensen and Paul Shepard in a work of ideological alchemy fuelled by the ancient universal esoteric beliefs found in Sufism, Taoism and hermeticism.

"The least pessimistic book I can recall reading. It brings anarchist resistance and the spirit together in a very wide-ranging and powerful contribution". John Zerzan, author of *Future Primitive* and *Running on Emptiness*.

"The book attempts no less than equipping contemporary anarchism with a footing that is often neglected: the transformation not only of society's structures but also of people's souls... an inspiring read". Gabriel Kuhn, author of *Life Under the Jolly Roger* and *Soccer vs the State*.

Also by Paul Cudenec

ANTIBODIES, ANARCHANGELS & OTHER ESSAYS

Antibodies, Anarchangels and Other Essays brings together a selection of work by Paul Cudenec in which he calls for a new deeper level of resistance to global capitalism – one which is rooted in the collective soul not just of humankind but of the living planet. He leads us along the intertwining environmental and philosophical strands of *Antibodies*, through the passion of *Anarchangels* and *The Task* and on to an informative analysis of Gladio, a state-terrorist branch of what he terms the "plutofascist" system. Also included, alongside short pieces on Taoism and Jungian psychology, is an interview with the author, in which he explains key aspects of his approach.

"Very readable and profoundly thoughtful... Many new insights on the destructive relationship between the greater part of humanity and the planet which tries to sustain them". Peter Marshall, author of *Demanding the Impossible: A History of Anarchism* and *Nature's Web: An Exploration of Ecological Thinking.*

MORE INFORMATION

To get in touch with Winter Oak please email
winteroak@greenmail.net or go to our website at
winteroak.org.uk. Paul Cudenec has a blog at
network23.org/paulcudenec and can be contacted via
cudenec@riseup.net

www.ingramcontent.com/pod-product-compliance
Lightning Source LLC
LaVergne TN
LVHW051411080426
835508LV00022B/3029